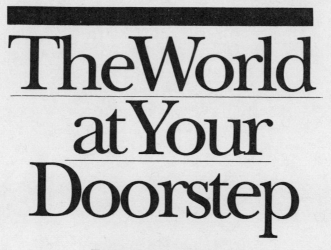

The World at Your Doorstep

Lawson Lau

A Handbook for International Student Ministry

INTERVARSITY PRESS
DOWNERS GROVE, ILLINOIS 60515

InterVarsity Press is the book-publishing division of Inter-Varsity Christian Fellowship, a student movement active on campus at hundreds of universities, colleges and schools of nursing. For information about local and regional activities, write IVCF, 233 Langdon St., Madison, WI 53703.

Distributed in Canada through InterVarsity Press, 860 Denison St., Unit 3, Markham, Ontario L3R 4H1, Canada.

Acknowledgment is made to Robert and Mary Taussig for permission to reproduce portions of Helping International Students Orientation Handbook.

Cover illustration: Roberta Polfus

ISBN 0-87784-526-3

Printed in the United States of America

Library of Congress Cataloging in Publication Data

Lau, Lawson.
    The world at your doorstep.

    Bibliography: p.
    1. Church work with foreign students—Handbooks,
manuals, etc.   I. Title.
BV1610.L34   1984   259'.24   84-19329
ISBN 0-87784-526-3

19	18	17	16	15	14	13	12	11	10	9	8	7	6	5	4	3	2	1
99	98	97	96	95	94	93	92	91	90	89	88	87	86	85	84			

To my father and mother
Mr. & Mrs. Lau Peng Sai
and
mother-in-law
Mrs. Loke Low Cheng
without whom I would not
have been an
international student

Foreword

There are rare instances when events and the gifts of people come together to meet the startling demands of the hour. We live in such a time. Recently there has been an unprecedented surge of internationals studying in other countries, especially in North America, for advanced education.

Many of these highly gifted and intelligent young people are destined to become leaders of the social, political, economic and spiritual structures of their nations. This lays a great challenge and burden upon the Christian church to become sensitive to the needs of these students while they are visitors. This will take leadership within the Christian community, people who will reach across cultural barriers to establish contact and offer loving friendship to these visitors.

Lawson Lau, a native of Singapore and former editor of *Impact* magazine in Singapore, has given us a vision for international student ministry by writing this book. Lau is an international student himself, having received a master's degree at Wheaton College in Wheaton, Illinois. He is currently a Ph.D. student at the University of Illinois at Urbana-Champaign.

This book provides a Christian understanding of the needs of the international student community. It also describes the unique opportunities and challenges international students bring to the Christian community in and near the campus. Most importantly, the book points the way for us to become involved during these crucial times for international student ministry.

Ned Hale
International Student Ministries Coordinator, IVCF

Introduction:
Opening Hearts and Doors to Internationals

When Chuan-Hsin Hsueh landed at Kansas City, Kansas, in February 1981, he had only thirty dollars in U.S. currency and "a little English."

He was alone. His wife and five children had remained in China.

As he could not afford a commuter plane, he took a bus to Manhattan, Kansas. A former research chemist at Beijing College of Chemical Engineering, forty-four-year-old Hsueh was headed for Kansas State University to pursue Ph.D. studies in chemistry. He arrived at 9:00 P.M. that winter night.

Sensing that this Chinese gentleman was a stranger, a Christian approached Hsueh at the bus stop and learned of his predicament. Hsueh knew no one in Manhattan and could not afford to pay for a hotel room. The Christian phoned Professor Robert Taussig of Kansas State University. Professor Taussig readily agreed to pick him up at the bus stop. Hsueh spent his first night in the United States in the home of a Christian couple.

A weary Hsueh did not wake up at the crack of dawn. After Professor Taussig had left for work the next morning, his wife,

Mary, had breakfast with Hsueh. Just before the meal Mary said, "I'm going to thank God for our food."

"God? Who is that?" asked Hsueh.

Months later Hsueh attended a Bible study group run by members of Grace Baptist Church, a church the Taussigs belong to. In halting English Hsueh said, "I like it [the Bible]. Some [scriptural] principles are good from my opinion."

International student Hsueh began his sojourn in the United States in an atmosphere of warmth by meeting Christians who have open hearts and open doors.

You Are Given a New Frontier

"Never in the history of the Christian church has a generation of Christians had a greater opportunity to reach the nations of the world than we in America have today," affirms a former staffworker with International Students, Inc.[1]

"If we believe in the sovereignty of God, then we need not doubt that God has brought them here to the United States for more than an education or mere social experience. God has a special purpose for his church and for these international visitors. As Christians, we have, by the grace of God, the most important reality of all to share with them. In the history of the world, nothing more important than the gospel of Christ was ever accomplished or proclaimed, and we have been entrusted with this singular, indispensable message for the evangelization of all mankind."

He points out that a great misunderstanding of missions today is that it is understood solely, or primarily, in terms of geography. "Rather," he contends, "in the truly biblical sense, missions is to be understood in terms of persons. The location is of secondary concern.

"Can we consistently claim that we are concerned about world evangelism when we are largely ignoring the transplanted foreign mission field which God has brought to us?"

Temporarily uprooted from familiar social, economic, cultural and religious surroundings, tens of thousands of international students are transplanted each year into the soil of colleges and universities in the United States. The frontiers of foreign missions are no longer only in Tibet, Saudi Arabia, Mongolia and China. They are also in Boston, New York, Chicago and Los Angeles, for they have come to the United States in the presence of international visitors.

"It has often been said that all Christians can have a part in foreign missions by praying, most by giving, but that only a few could do the going. However, God has now made it possible for virtually every Christian in the United States to actually be a foreign missionary.

"How can we possibly estimate the potential effect of these millions of internationals on the whole missionary enterprise around the world in the next twenty-five years? And yet, lamentably, less than one-fourth of a per cent of these internationals are being effectively reached at present."

The ministry among internationals in the United States is "one of the most neglected mission fields in the world. . . . Less than half a per cent of all the Protestant missionaries in the world are working among these people, and yet it is one of the greatest missionary opportunities of the century."

The majority of international visitors in the United States, including students, "are destined in the next twenty-five years to occupy one-fourth to one-half of the world's top positions of leadership—politically, militarily, economically, scientifically, academically and socially."

Working in this new frontier in missions has several advantages: "All of these people speak English, so if you want to go to minister to them, you will not have to learn another language. This means that your missionary activity among them can begin immediately. Furthermore, you will not have any problems with visas and government restrictions. There is total religious freedom.

"Another advantage lies in the fact that almost no adjustment to food or to climate will be required of you. The people of whom I speak are friendly, polite and hospitable. And, perhaps most remarkable of all in our day, they like Americans and want them to be their friends. They are delighted to visit your home, as well as to have you in theirs—and it is rare to find any of them who do not love children.

"The vast majority of them are diligent, serious-minded and ambitious. Many of them are eager to know about the Christian faith and most of them will accept a Bible and read it. An impressive number of them are willing to spend hours talking about the Christian faith with those who show a sincere interest in them."

The parting question is: "As you see these strangers from other lands, I ask you, What is your attitude toward the Lord Jesus who has brought them among us?"

A Collage of Intellectuals
Foreign faces have a common characteristic. They are foreign. Unlike the distinctive individualism of the local face, foreign faces merge into one another. "I see men," says the man at Bethsaida. "But they look like trees, walking" (Mk 8:24). Like him we may need a second touch from Christ to perceive international students as men and women, not walking trees.

Diversity, not homogeneity, is a mark of the international student population. This should be kept in mind throughout this book although international students are discussed as one category of students. Culture and costumes, foods, languages, religions differentiate one student from another. Personal mannerisms, physique, English accent compound the differences.

The United States hosted almost one-third of the 842,705 international students in forty-five countries in 1978.[2] Its total of 263,940 students is more than twice that of the second-largest host country, France (108,286). South and East Asia send more students to the United States than any other region. Iran, Taiwan, Nigeria and Venezuela are the leading countries. Seventy colleges and universities throughout the United States have more than a thousand foreign students. (See Appendix C for more information.)

Students who come to know Christ while in the United States may well be an asset to their home churches. Their potential for sharing the gospel among their own people is immeasurable. They already know the language and culture and have their circles of friends. And they are certainly treated with less suspicion and distrust than is often given to foreign missionaries in this age.

Ancient Chinese Custom

Before proceeding further I think it appropriate to observe an old tradition in Chinese scholarship—the writer of a treatise owes his readers an initial account of himself. It serves to orient readers to the viewpoints they are about to encounter. My interest in international students began on August 31, 1980, when I left my home country, Singapore, for the United States. That essentially was the day I became an international student. I had a working life of more than fourteen years—as a teacher, a lieutenant in the army, a journalist and a magazine editor—before arriving at Wheaton College in Illinois as an undergraduate. I graduated sixteen months later. I was a literature major. After another sixteen months I graduated with a master's degree in communications from Wheaton College Graduate School. I am now studying at the University of Illinois at Urbana-Champaign. My sojourn in the United States and the writing of this book are enthusiastically shared by another international student. My wife, Pamela, is a graduate student in philosophy at the University of Chicago, has completed her course work and is now working on her dissertation out of residence. Andreana, who officially joined us at Mercy Hospital, Urbana, Illinois on September 18, 1983, has enlarged our fields of study without bestowing us with additional time.

I felt a passion for sharing my experiences as an international student after being in the United States for only a few months. A sizeable portion of this book is therefore autobiographical. But I have also received much help from many peo-

ple through interviews, reading their writings and the encouragement of friends and professors, some of whom read this
book in its first draft. Reverend James Reapsome and Mr. Harry
Genet paved the way for me to meet Dr. and Mrs. Robert
Taussig. Professor John Gration gave me the idea of how to
structure the book. Professor Glenn Arnold has been of
considerable blessing to me both as a professor and a brother
in Christ. Those who have demonstrated a steadfast interest in
international students and in the writing of this book also
include Mr. and Mrs. Hal Guffey and Mr. Ned Hale.

The main purpose of this book is to encourage positive
interaction among American Christians and international
students. Part One deals with tensions that may arise when
international students find themselves thrust into a new
cultural environment and discusses how these tensions may be
resolved. The principles discussed are also of value to Americans going overseas, or for international students in most
countries. Sharing the good news with international students in
a spirit of sensitivity is the key exhortation in Part Two.
Although there is a growing awareness among American
Christians of the need to minister to international students in
the United States, there are those who have a long-standing
commitment to this category of humanity. My choice of the
Taussigs as a "model" couple is circumstantial. Nevertheless,
chapter eight shows that they have done much to merit our
attention. Appendix A provides a biblical perspective on
ministering to international students. Appendix B gives
information on organizations involved with international
students so readers can obtain further assistance or materials
on how to start or upgrade a ministry to international students.
Appendix C provides statistics on the numbers, distribution and
countries of international students.

Psalm 96 captures in a most magnificent way several major
concerns of this book. Vibrant, teeming with praise, consumed
by an international rather than a national outlook, moved by
an overwhelming desire to praise the Lord, the psalmist was led

by the Spirit of God to express, freely and creatively, both his
feelings and his thoughts:

O sing to the LORD a new song;
  sing to the LORD, all the earth!
Sing to the LORD, bless his name;
  tell of his salvation from day to day.
Declare his glory among the nations,
  his marvelous works among all the peoples!
For great is the LORD, and greatly to be praised;
  he is to be feared above all gods. . . .
Say among the nations, "The LORD reigns!
  Yea, the world is established, it shall never be moved;
  he will judge the peoples with equity."
Let the heavens be glad, and let the earth rejoice;
  let the sea roar, and all that fills it;
  let the field exult, and everything in it!
Then shall all the trees of the wood sing for joy
  before the LORD, for he comes,
  for he comes to judge the earth.
He will judge the world with righteousness,
  and the peoples with his truth.

PART 1:

BRIDGES TO UNDERSTANDING

CHAPTER 1

ADJUSTING TO
A NEW CULTURE

MY FIRST WEEK ON A UNITED STATES CAMPUS WAS BOTH MAR-
velous and bewildering. I could have been on Lewis's Perelan-
dra. When I was transported through space and entered the
United States, I assumed "alien" immigration status. I was
effectively cut off from a land and people I had known for more
than thirty years. Even my wife of a year was not with me. I was
no longer a member of a majority ethnic group. I was a distinct
minority.

I was an alien.

I felt almost as "alone, alone, all all alone" as Coleridge's
ancient mariner. I didn't have an albatross hung round my
neck, it is true, but I bore the unmistakable mark of a foreigner
in need of hospitality. I had flown a long distance and came
to rest on a continent floating between the Atlantic and Pacific
Oceans, isolated from the rest of the wide, wide world. On
second thought, would *I* be the albatross? But everything was
still too strange, too wondrous, too rarified for my heart and

soul to be weighed down by tension or agony.

It was a privilege to be here in the United States. I was most conscious of this fact. I had worked for more than fourteen years and now was back in school—as a full-time student. It was a strange feeling in a new land.

Outpatient Treatment for Culture Shock

I did not anticipate culture shock. My experiences suggested that I was well prepared to enter the American scene. Several reasons gave me the confidence that I could adapt to life in the United States without too much hassle. Two of them concerned language and society.

Although I lived in a predominantly Chinese nation, I communicated primarily in English as Singapore, like the United States, was a British colony. Singapore is a pluralistic society, and I had come into close contact with people of different religions and races. A senior British Royal Artillery officer was my immediate superior when I was a second lieutenant in the Singapore Armed Forces. I had no problems relating to or communicating with him.

As editor of *Singapore Crusade Times* I had worked for six months with Henry Holley and his son, Hank, both staff members of the Billy Graham Evangelistic Association. I easily understood evangelist Billy Graham's accent during the Singapore Billy Graham Crusade in December 1978.

I had a further advantage over most international students. My destination in the United States was Wheaton, Illinois. My Singapore office was located in Bible House. It is a building occupied by more than ten Christian organizations. So for more than three years prior to my arrival in the United States, I worked in a miniature Wheaton.

Under such circumstances I hardly acknowledged that I was a culture shock victim. Now, as I reflect on what it means to face culture shock, I am inclined to confess that I too had been a victim. Perhaps not one who needed intensive care, but certainly one who required gentle outpatient treatment.

A helpful definition of culture shock is provided by anthropologist Kalervo Oberg. He states that culture shock is precipitated by the anxiety that results from losing all our familiar signs and symbols of social intercourse. These signs or cues include the thousand and one ways we orient ourselves to the situations of daily life. They tell us when to shake hands and what to say when we meet people, when and how to give tips, how to give orders to servants, how to make purchases, when to accept or refuse invitations, when to take statements seriously and when not. These cues, which may be words, gestures, facial expressions, customs or norms, are acquired by all of us in the course of growing up and are as much a part of our culture as the language we speak or the beliefs we accept.[1]

A change in these cues can result in physical discomfort. Two Hong Kong students, for instance, were initiated into how not to use the bedspread when they were guests of an American family. After a day of activities their American hostess showed them to the guest room and bade them good night. The lovely room was near perfection except for one detail. Blankets were usually folded and placed at the foot of the bed in their home in Hong Kong. There was no sign of any blanket in the guest room.

These Americans are strange people, they thought. Here we are in their home on a winter night and they don't provide us with blankets!

Their cultural upbringing required them to remain silent. It would be impolite of them to ask their hostess for blankets, as it would imply her inhospitality. So the two of them spent an uncomfortable night sleeping on the bedspread, mistaking it for the sheet.

Culture shock has also been described as "that emotional disturbance which results from adjustments to new cultural environment."[2] An African student, newly arrived in the United States, attended an American church and met with culture shock. During the service the pastor enthusiastically introduced a young missionary girl who had just returned from the mission field and was to share her experience. He then hugged her and kissed her on the cheek. This was intimacy far in excess of the cultural norms of the African. He sought help from his American student adviser the next morning. He said, "I couldn't believe my eyes. I was so utterly shocked. Could you explain it to me?" He said his wife and children were with him and he could not explain the odd phenomenon to them.[3]

That Helpless Minority Feeling

My wife and I have noticed that Americans who have lived abroad usually relate much better to us than those who have not. A multiplicity of reasons could account for our observations. One is that they too have experienced culture shock. They have tasted of life in a foreign country where they were an ethnic minority. They could empathize with us.

Japan and the United States are contrasting nations. One is homogeneous and the other is pluralistic. A White or Black American living in Japan forms part of an ethnic minority. So too a Japanese student on a United States campus. It may be as enlightening to examine the experience of one as the other. But the former may heighten the contrast.

Professor Stephen Franklin of Wheaton College Graduate School is broad-shouldered, stands head and shoulders above the average Japanese, and sports a red beard.[4] Two other factors made him an even more prominent specimen of a foreign culture during his five-year sojourn in Japan. First, he and his family were the only White residents in an area of about twenty-five thousand people. Second, his red hair and beard conveyed a silent but potent message. Japanese mythology depicts demons as red-haired. So even the simple act of taking a stroll down a street became a circus show.

"Wherever I went," says Professor Franklin, "people would be staring at me." This was usually done discreetly. "The Japanese are very careful not to embarrass you. So they would walk by me without looking at me. But very often after I walked by they would turn around and stare at me. So if I wanted to embarrass them, I could turn on my heels real quick and catch a whole line of gaping faces."

Children, however, were less polite. "Little children would turn to their mothers, punch them and say, 'Hey! An outsider! Hey! An outsider!' It's a rather impolite type of expression."

Living in such a non-American culture could be oppressive for an American who does not care for celebrity status. "That can really bear down on a person's soul," says Franklin. "Day after day, month after month, year after year. In a way that, for instance, I did not feel when I was in Singapore. I am different. People looked at me. But there was a lot of awfully funny-looking people from other countries there, too, some of them looking a lot more queer than I look."

Culture shock, however, is not confined to cultures as manifestly contrasting as the American-Japanese example. An American in France can run into as much emotional discomfort, sometimes over apparently insignificant matters. William Smalley, editor of *Practical Anthropology,* narrates his experience on the French habit of shaking hands. It happened when he was in Paris to study French. Like most Americans he found it difficult to know when and where to shake hands. The French people seemed to be shaking hands all the time. "We felt silly shaking our hands so much," writes Smalley.[5]

The Americans reacted by circulating stories to emphasize the "queerness" of such a French custom. One told of how French children shake hands with their parents before going to bed every night. "The small and inconsequential difference of habit in shaking hands was enough to bring uneasiness," observes Smalley, "and combined with hundreds of other uncertainties brought culture shock to many."[6]

The following are some of the symptoms of culture shock that an American goes through in a new culture: excessive washing of hands; excessive concern over drinking water, food, dishes and bedding; an absent-minded, faraway stare; a feeling of helplessness and a desire for dependence on long-term residents of his own nationality; fits of anger over delays and other minor frustrations; delay and outright refusal to learn the language of the host country; great concern over minor pains and eruptions of the skin; and that terrible longing to be back home, to be able to have a good cup of coffee and a piece of apple pie.[7] Many of these symptoms are applicable to the international student coming to the United States.

The Four Faces of the Victim

Oberg identifies four phases of culture shock that people may go through.[8] The first is fascination. A misty glow envelops their eyes, and a benign smile lingers in the corners of their mouths. This honeymoon stage may last from a few days or weeks to six months. For most international students this stage is woefully brief.

Important people from other countries, however, are treated graciously and politely by those trained to relate to foreigners and who speak their language. They are pampered by their hosts, who act as buffers between them and the frustrations or grievances that come with living in a foreign land. These are well-to-do tourists for all practical purposes. If their visit terminates at this stage, they return home to speak glowingly of their pleasant, if superficial, experience overseas.

This feeling of well-being usually takes a plunge if the foreign visitors prolong their stay. They come into direct contact with the strangeness of their surroundings. They have to cope with real conditions of life. They develop a hostile and aggressive attitude toward the host country at this stage. Their eyes may grow cynical and cold, and they may sneer in contempt at those around them.

International students find that the pleasures of orientation are replaced by the pressures of academic life. Other tensions surface. They may not obtain as much academic credit for work done in their home country as they anticipated. Financial sponsors may be slow in sending funds, and their college or university may threaten expulsion because of their failure to fulfill their monetary obligations. Examinations and term papers besiege them. Conflicts of interest may appear between them and their American roommates. As trials mount they feel that their new American friends are unsympathetic or indifferent to their troubles. The help friends offer is inadequate to deal with the students' escalating sense of frustration. The international students' summary judgment of Americans is: "We just don't like them."

At this second stage international students need intensive care, but may not obtain it. They are culture-shock victims. They reject their host country and its people. They band together with other international students to grouse about the United States. Subjective, derogatory, emotionally charged stereotypes of Americans may be used. International students also regress. Their home countries suddenly assume exaggerated importance. Only the positive aspects of home are recalled. These are also symptoms of the culture-shock disease. If international students are cured, they stay. If not, it is best for them to leave the United States before they suffer a nervous breakdown. Oberg observes that some people cannot cope with living in foreign countries.

The key that unlocks the third stage of culture shock for international students is a working knowledge of English and an ability to get around by themselves. They are no longer spectators in orientation programs. They are oriented. Their troubles are not completely over. But they have taken enough punches to know how to ward off or return blows. Their sense of humor is restored. Their eyes take on an occasional twinkle, and self-confident grins may unexpectedly break forth. Instead of criticizing, they joke about the United States and their own difficulties. They adopt a superior attitude to the Americans. They also know there are poor devils in a worse state, and they can offer help to other international students. They are no longer uninitiated tyros. They are off the danger list, on the way to recovery.

In the fourth stage the students' adjustment is as complete as it can be. Their appearance returns to normal. They are cured.

They accept the customs of the United States as just another way of living. They operate within their new environment without anxiety, except for moments of strain. Only with a complete grasp of all the cues of social interaction will this strain disappear. They understand what Americans are saying but they are not always sure what Americans mean. Nuances may still elude them. With a complete adjustment they not only accept the foods, habits and customs, but actually begin to enjoy them. When they return home, they may take souvenirs back with them. They miss the United States and its people to whom they have grown accustomed.

The Americanization of the Student

It is normal to be overpowered by uneasiness on entering a new culture. This is because the unfamiliar environment reduces foreigners to the status of babies—awkward, physically overgrown babies. Oberg's four phases of culture shock provide a helpful bridge to understanding students' adjustment throes. Louis Luzbetak, who carried out field work in anthropology and linguistics in New Guinea, modifies phase two and gives us another useful perspective.[9]

International students in the second stage of culture shock may take one of two routes to overcome their frustration. One is that which Oberg suggests. The students reject the United States and its people. Luzbetak suggests the other. It is "going native." International students completely identify with their American counterparts. They experience a neurotic longing for security and an exaggerated hunger for belonging, an unbalanced craving for acceptance. This drives the students to indiscriminately approve and accept as their own virtually all American ways and values. International students who live with ethnocentric American students are especially vulnerable to this method of becoming "acceptable."

They usually begin by extolling beyond merit the religious, moral and cultural environment that is causing the shock. Before long, inordinately close friendships with American families or individuals are formed. The hunger for belonging keeps gnawing within them while their own culture looms like an insurmountable wall between them and those they want to be fully accepted by.

This route is more likely to be taken by students who are still very malleable, particularly unmarried teen-agers. It is also seen in the students' young children. They go native without any qualms.

Going native is different from identification with a new culture. Students feel compelled to go native to overcome cultural and social tensions. They may unconsciously do so to escape rejection by their American counterparts. It is a manifestation of a wish for self-survival. They discard their former ways of thinking, feeling, speaking and doing things in favor of the ways and values of their American friends. And they are often critical of students from their own country who have not gone native.

On the other hand, healthy identification with the American culture involves empathy and adoption of selected American ways and values. Empathy requires a sympathetic understanding of the American way of life. Such students understand and appreciate the reasons behind why Americans behave, think and react as they do. Adoption involves internal approval and external usage of American ways and values. This acculturation process is based on reason and prudence rather than a rationalization process. Identification does not aim at acceptance or belonging for its own sake.

International students who have gone native will run headlong into a fresh set of problems when they return home. Their American accents and values will come into conflict with those in their home countries.

Recovery through Self-Discovery
International students who come for graduate studies in the United States are usually intelligent and mature. Some could have held responsible governmental positions in their home

countries with professional, social and economic status. Their symbols of authority, however, are forfeited when they enter the United States as students. This is exacerbated if they lack proficiency in English. They are unable to show their education and intelligence. They respond to their American counterparts like handicapped persons—which they are. They fumble over the simplest of social intercourse. This state of confusion and suffering is debilitating. They feel like fools because they seem to act foolish. This painful phase of culture shock nevertheless has the potential for paving the way to recovery through self-discovery.

Smalley suggests that self-discovery sometimes comes in the frank facing of utter defeat.[10] The teacher who is so highly respected in her home country, the pastor from a large and influential church, the head of a government department—they each lose their social status when they arrive on the United States campus and enter language school. The teacher may find that someone just out of high school does better in language study than she. Or the pastor's wife, who always laughed at herself because she was so scatterbrained and did average work in college, makes far better progress than he. Both the teacher and pastor feel utterly humiliated. Their long record of success is broken. People accustomed to success will find it hard to take this unexpected shock.

They can, however, avoid giving in to despair because everyone can learn. They can determine to do their best in spite of the difficulties and study hard. They can refuse to give in to the symptoms of culture shock. They can surmount them by developing bilingualism and biculturalism. They may find the pace to be slower than they would like it to be, but they can persevere.

In their state of disorientation students may sometimes discover their own emotional insecurity. They find themselves behaving childishly, giving vent to temper tantrums over trifles, projecting their problems on others. Only when they face their insecurity can they learn to approach their problems more rationally and to work systematically toward a resolution of their difficulties. They can then adopt a healthy outlook of themselves and their situation. They can thus recover from culture shock through the process of self-discovery.

For Christian students it may be a time of renewed commitment to Christ. Even as the realities of the barriers to cross-cultural communication depress them, they realize that their presence in the United States is not a mere accident. They see their language throes in the perspective of the larger ministry they are called to. They may determine afresh, and perhaps in a more realistic way than ever before, to commit themselves and their weaknesses to Christ. The symptoms of rejection and insecurity are replaced by an objective knowledge of their own strengths and weaknesses. With this knowledge comes a relaxed acceptance of themselves.

Of Earthy Smells and Heavenly Scents

People who have grown up in one particular culture seldom perceive their own cultural idiosyncrasies. It is only when East meets West that such cultural oddities are brought into sharp scrutiny. These cultural traits may amuse, astound, perplex or frustrate.

A bottle of English Leather aftershave lotion is the extent of my worldly goods in the realm of unnatural scents. On the other hand, I know of American students who invest a tidy sum of money in an array of deodorants, colognes and scents.

Body odor is a delicate issue. Dr. Robert Taussig, who welcomed Chuan-Hsin Hsueh to Kansas State, is, as a professor of veterinary medicine, among the more qualified persons to address this subject of earthy smells and heavenly scents.[11] He says, "Africans traditionally don't pay close attention to body odors. But Americans are completely decided that anyone who is at all civilized is going for the underarm deodorant. An African comes into his home and the American is offended because of his body odor. We have learned that Africans are perfectly willing to use deodorants, but no one has ever talked to them about it. So we freely share it with the Africans. We say something like this: 'Americans are very strange people and they think that all people should use deodorant on their bodies after they bathe.' And the African usually says, 'Well, I'm glad to do this. Where do I buy it?' "

I usually bathe twice a day. When I first heard that some American students don't bathe every day, I wondered what impact they would make on my sense of smell. Then I noticed that some may not even bathe after they go jogging. They just liberally spray their favorite scent over the sweat and grime.

Eugene Nida, a specialist in linguistics and anthropological studies, provides another viewpoint. He writes,

> Judgments critical of the white man are not solely the result of failure to appreciate our way of life or our habits. For one thing, we as members of the white race often have a very obnoxious odor, in other words, B.O. It is true that other races also have characteristic odors, but in general offensiveness we are probably the greatest "stinkers." (Anyone unconvinced of this should go on a hot day into a poorly ventilated locker room in a large gymnasium.) The Thai people were utterly shocked to get hygiene books published in America saying that one should take a bath at least once a week. A Thai who does not bathe twice a day is not regarded as fit for human society. Some Oriental students in America have had to get separate rooms because they simply could not stand the offensive odor of their roommates.[12]

Another Awful Odor
Body odor isn't the only nasal irritant in crosscultural togetherness. Cooking odors may be equally offensive to some Americans.

Karen Greiff, a secretary in the graduate school at Wheaton, told me of a Singaporean girl who came after the fall term began. Thus the school could not provide housing for her. My wife, Pamela, and I volunteered our assistance. Pam and I met Paik-Kah Wu at O'Hare Airport in Chicago, and she stayed with us several days. In the meantime Pam tried to obtain off-campus housing for Paik-Kah. The first American landlady Pam telephoned had one overriding question: "What are your friend's cooking and eating habits?" She had had a previous tenant, a Korean girl, "who seemed to be cooking the whole day, and the smell of the cooking filled the whole house." The landlady didn't appreciate the odor. Pam was astounded by this aversion to aromas which are for us a part of life.

Paik-Kah settled for another American landlady who did not ask about her cooking and eating habits. Jean, the landlady, was very friendly. When Paik-Kah returned from her first shopping trip laden with groceries and produce, Jean helped to put them away in her allotted section of their shared refrigerator. Then Jean's eyes alighted on some green onions. "Please wrap them in plastic," she requested. Paik-Kah bought fresh garlic on her next shopping trip. Garlic is an essential ingredient in Chinese cooking. Jean asked that Paik-Kah switch to the less aromatic powdered garlic. Even then Jean would quietly retire to her room and close the door each time Paik-Kah did any cooking.

Most Asian girls and women take pride in their cooking. To ask them to alter their cooking habits or style is to seek a major change.

The American's New Clothes

"Naked come to Thee for dress" is a line of a hymn that acknowledges our utter dependence on God's provision. We enter and leave the world with nothing. This fact, however, does not deter us from harboring an acquisitive spirit. It usually includes the desire for a wardrobe.

"The Emperor's New Clothes" is a tale of how an emperor's obsession for new clothes led him into a foolish situation. Clothes and the lack of clothes continue to be a source of either embarrassment or misunderstanding in the modern world. It is often heightened when contrasting cultures meet.

Untouched by Western civilization there are tribal people whose women do not cover their breasts. A cover story in the

December 1982 issue of *Time* illustrates this.[13]

Should a missionary ask the women to wear blouses? The church leaders in the Ngbaka church in northern Congo were unanimous in objecting to such a request by a missionary. "We are not going to have our wives dress like prostitutes," protested an elder. In that part of the Congo the well-dressed and fully dressed African women were too often prostitutes. They usually had the money to spend on clothes.[14]

African students in the United States may run into another kind of misunderstanding. One African student was angry that his American church friends brought him old clothes. His reaction was, "Why do you bring me your old leftover clothes? If I am truly a guest in your country, why don't you bring me new clothes?" His friends thought they were doing him a favor by providing him with free warm clothes for the Illinois winter. Another African student was annoyed by Americans who asked him to dress in his national costume when attending functions. He said, "Our clothes are so thin that it is very uncomfortable for us to walk around in them when it is so cold here."

College girls face a variation of the same theme. A Taiwanese graduate student avoided going to a dressy American church. "They all competed with each other over who has the latest fashion," she said. Her small budget for clothes made her appear shabby. She felt embarrassed in the presence of American girls who were so fashionably dressed, all in their Sunday best.

Adjusting to a new culture is like admiring the shoreline of Lake Michigan and then to suddenly wake up in its icy water. I certainly felt an initial sense of exhilaration before the numbness of naked vulnerability set in. What I and all internationals need are people willing to warm and comfort us as we enter an otherwise chilly environment.

CHAPTER 2

ACADEMIC AND SOCIAL NEEDS

AS A NEWLY ARRIVED INTERNATIONAL STUDENT MY MAJOR NEEDS fell into two basic categories. First, orientation to life in the United States. Second, orientation to the academic requirements of the college.

My primary reason for coming to the United States was to fulfill a long-standing wish for academic and professional training. Although I had more than six years of experience in journalistic work, I had hardly any formal instruction. Such training would, I believed, upgrade my writing skills and my teaching of creative writing. The only university in my country does not have a journalism school or a communications department. The United States offers excellent programs in these spheres.

International students may come to the United States for many other reasons. Nevertheless, the desire to acquire a college, university or professional degree is almost always the chief aim.

African or Asian students seldom leave their countries for studies abroad unnoticed. It is normal to have a sendoff party at their home airport with a couple dozen people or more. Their parents, brothers and sisters, close and distant relatives, and friends would all be there. Close communal ties in African or Asian countries render the departure of one of their members for studies in some distant land a gala affair. With such a rousing sendoff, it would be a nightmare to have to return home without a degree or, preferably, degrees. Academic success means honor and material rewards. Failure is a shameful admission of inadequacy. It is deemed a waste of time, money, effort—a stigma of communal proportions. A *Time* article notes that "Asian Americans are only about 1.5% of the U.S. population, but what they lack in numbers they make up for in achievement. Out of 40 Westinghouse finalists, nine were born in Asia and three others were of Asian descent. Some 10% of Harvard's freshman class is Asian American. . . . Most Asians regard education as the best avenue to recognition and success."[1]

Since academic success is vital, an understanding of academic procedures, requirements and regulations is a strongly felt need. Then there is the need to function in a new educational system. The pressure to perform in a short time after arrival is intensified by the fast pace of academic life in the American educational system. Loneliness adds to the throes of adjustment.

Inside an Academic Space Mountain

Now that I have experienced a roller-coaster ride in Disneyland's Space Mountain, I am intrigued by striking similarities between the ride and my first academic quarter in a United States college.

Both began with a marked carnival atmosphere. Pleasant orientation activities, mainly socials, occupied my attention during the week before the start of academic work. They helped to ease the pain of separation from loved ones. The warm late-summer weather enhanced the hazy, carefree atmosphere. Like the seemingly endless queue leading to a piece of action in Space Mountain, anticipation ran high.

I received an orientation brochure on entering Disneyland. Similarly, in college I was given a neatly compiled package of materials designed for incoming students. It contained academic and other information on the college, coupons for use in nearby stores, community information, maps of my immediate surroundings. I also had a name tag for orientation week. It was a useful advertisement. It authorized me to look lost without social penalty and it permitted the natives around me to initiate a rescue attempt.

There were, of course, intimations of reality ahead. The college calendar clearly stated when classes were to begin and when examinations week was. It was like the prominently displayed signs at Space Mountain. The would-be participant was informed to turn back if he or she had a weak heart or other ailments that might render it dangerous to ride the roller coaster. But, to most beginners, warning signs are given as much heed as some motherly advice. I was one such beginner.

A drastic change of pace characterized the next stage. I found myself sitting in a car moving into the inner darkness of Space Mountain. A flashing red light in front during the initial slow uphill climb forewarned of a new phase of life. Then came the long plunge into nothingness. Sharp turns at high speed were next. Unpleasant moments came when I thought I would be thrown off the car. *Will I survive this ride?* A couple of screams from somewhere around me was the reply. It was too late to turn back.

In a similar track, my second week on campus began on Monday with an uphill task to get registered. The registration procedure appeared to be unduly complex. I was a lost sheep among stern shepherds.

Classes began on Tuesday. Some inner force overcame summer inertia and propelled me from classroom to classroom. And in these caldrons of learning, syllabi and examination schedules were unleashed like some endless tropical thunder-storm. Mentally buffeted, I plodded back to my apartment. With a red pen I marked the examination dates on my calendar. When I finished, there seemed to be more red than the original blue. I did not recall being so inundated before. By Friday my spirits fell so low that I felt as though I was dragging them along somewhere behind me in the rain and the wind and the mud.

Just as fleeting moments of respite occurred on the roller coaster, one of these came at the end of the week. Saturday saw the ceremonial dedication of the Billy Graham Center, located on the Wheaton campus. My spirits were partially restored as two of my Singaporean friends, Peter Chao and John Ng, were there for the ceremony. They stayed in my apartment over the weekend. After two weeks when I could not talk intelligibly to anyone about Singapore, it felt good to chat about home.

One disappointment during my first week came from the college registrar. He told me it would take five or six years to obtain both my bachelor's and master's degrees, though the graduate admissions director had written me in Singapore that it would only take three. He said, however, that I could seek credit for work I had done back home. So in the third week, after receiving copies of my transcripts, I began the arduous task of making appointments and visiting the chairmen of five departments in the college. I was still discouraged to have to register as a college freshman with advanced standing.

I was apprehensive. Would they be sympathetic toward an international student who had studied in a different education-al system? Very few Americans I had met had even heard of Singapore.[2] What are the criteria for granting credit? What should I say when questioned on the content of my courses? I had completed them between eight and twelve years earlier. Much was learned and much forgotten. As it turned out, my fears were unfounded. Without exception, all the professors treated me with a dignity and understanding I had not anticipated.

My misgivings, however, had started in the registrar's office.

A portentous skit during orientation week should have alerted me. In it a transfer student hesitantly approached the registrar and said she was a junior transfer. The registrar looked her up and down nonchalantly, and brusquely said, "O.K., I'll take you in as a sophomore!" He then indicated that the interview was over by shuffling some papers on his improvised table. The audience roared. It was hilarious. I should have known that the skit was not based on sheer fancy. Before I could visit the department chairmen, I needed authorization slips from the registrar. When I sought his approval for a year of Intermediate Laws credits from the University of London, England, his instant reply was, "I know. You want to get over to graduate school as quickly as possible, right?" His tone was uncannily similar to that of the registrar in the skit. Or was it vice versa? His conjecture was, of course, correct. I was merely seeking what I thought was granted me before coming to the United States.

Sixteen months later at my graduation dinner he said, "Congratulations, Lawson!" as he shook me by the hand. He could be a nice guy after all.[3]

My first taste of the American examination system came at the end of that same third week. The American system is unlike Singapore's, where tests given through the year do not count toward the final grade. Only the examinations at the end of the nine-month academic year are considered. My first test was a red-blooded all-American quiz. A Greek quiz. I was still struggling over the alphabet! My spirits plunged to their lowest level yet. They lay there for many weeks.

All good things, it is said, come to an end. Mercifully, bad things also have their day. The roller coaster ground to a halt. So did my first quarter. My shaken senses were adequately intact for me to realize that I had survived an elemental journey through inner space.

A Catalog of Problems
I did not understand the concept of an American liberal arts

education when I arrived in the United States. Singapore's
educational system is basically British and does not have a liberal arts structure. One of my professors raised a puzzled eye-
brow when he perceived my ignorance. "But it's in the catalog,"
he pointed out with a touch of incredulity. His next remark
indicated the drift of his concern. "Weren't you given a copy
of the catalog?"

"Yes, I was," I said sheepishly. It had traveled halfway round
the world to Singapore, and I had dutifully brought it right back
to its homeland.

"All the requirements," he said, "are explained in the
catalog."

I gave as intelligent a series of nods as I could muster.

"Why don't you read it over, and then if you have any
questions you can ask me about them?"

It was a sensible suggestion. Surely I could understand a
simple catalog. The campus was, moreover, swarming with
students bristling with thorny questions. I would be discourte-
ous to monopolize a professor's time when he had so many
students demanding attention. Even the evangelist Philip, I
thought, might not be able to function efficiently or effectively
if he were confronted by a dozen Ethiopian eunuchs crowded
into a single chariot, each reading a different Scripture portion.
What, then, with lesser mortals?

Back in the quiet of my college apartment (I was then living
alone—my wife was to join me three months later), I pored over
the catalog as meticulously as I would an Internal Revenue
Service document. Both have much in common. They spawn
frustration. I seemed to have enough questions to overload a
computer. I soon met another Singaporean student who had
arrived on the campus nearly two years previously and was then
similarly perplexed. Peh-Cheng Ng unraveled the intricacies of
the catalog and the educational system. Once understood, the
contents of the catalog seemed almost ludicrously simple.

After sixteen months I graduated from college and went to
graduate school. The transition was easy. I understood what

catalog terms such as *departmental prerequisites, general education requirements, required courses* and *electives* meant. It was like crossing the six-foot wall during my boot camp days in the Singapore army. The first attempt was the most difficult. Each crossing made the next one easier—for me. But there were always those who confronted the obstacle for the very first time.

I was working as a graduate assistant when a first-year Korean graduate student asked me about making an appointment with his professor for academic advising. He also showed me his Program Planning Guide. He carried the minimum load of twelve hours for a full-time student. Eight hours were for graduate credit, and four went toward a noncredit prerequisite for a graduate course to be taken at a later date. I volunteered the information that he was getting only eight hours of graduate credit for the current semester. We were then two-thirds through the semester.

"No," he countered. "Twelve."

I explained the difference between a noncredit prerequisite course and a graduate course taken for credit. He was perturbed. Being an Asian I understood his hesitancy over accepting my explanation. For most of us, professors are the authority figures. Their word is law. I suggested that he seek clarification from his adviser. He readily agreed.

When we next met, he grimaced, clenched his fist, struck his chest and said, "I'm very angry."

A Central American friend who was with us consoled him: "But you have learned a lot from the course, right?"

Such optimism was not out of place, but it did not remove the Korean's grounds for anger. He was in financial straits. And he had paid more than five hundred dollars in tuition for a sixteen-week course under the impression that he was obtaining graduate credit. He could have fulfilled his prerequisite at a nearby community college at less than one hundred dollars for an eleven-week course.

International students who fly into the United States and plunge headlong into a weblike American educational system

for the first time need help. Without assistance they may fall
prey to unnecessary frustration.

English: A Perplexing Language

Language, I thought, won't be a barrier for me. As a magazine
editor I had reviewed numerous books written by Americans.
Nevertheless, American English continues to intrigue me. I am
not merely referring to distinct differences in accent, pronun-
ciation and meaning. My first encounter with an American
oddity occurred at the Los Angeles International Airport where
I made a transit stop on my first day in the United States. I am
familiar with terms such as *loo, w.c., bathroom, lavatory, toilet,
gents.* But *rest room* stumped me. My immediate reaction was that
these North Americans are living up to my preconceived image
of them. They really know how to luxuriate in comfort! They
even have conveniently located rooms where the weary traveler
can take a rest. Images of spacious and tastefully decorated
rooms furnished with cozy beds drifted into my imagination. I
made no attempt to verify my conjectures, although I was tired.
As I sat in a corridor opposite a rest room, however, I gradually
figured out that my knowledge of synonyms was being enlarged.

Proficiency in English is a problem for most international
students. A report of the Education and World Affairs
Committee on Foreign Student Affairs states, "A number of
educators who have considerable experience with foreign
student problems estimate that about a third of the students
from underdeveloped areas do not have sufficient command of
the English language upon arrival in the United States to
enable them to grasp the substance of the regular lectures in
undergraduate or graduate courses."[4]

Most colleges and universities in the United States stipulate
a Test of English as a Foreign Language (TOEFL) score of 450-
550 as an entrance requirement for international students.
Even this is not foolproof. "We have discovered that the TOEFL
test," says Professor Julius Scott, "really makes very little

difference. Someone can rank very highly on the TOEFL test and be functionally a non-English speaker as far as our classrooms are concerned."[5]

Scott suggests two reasons for this lack of facility with the language. One, "because of the speed with which we speak." This is a valid observation. I have noticed that Midwesterners are usually in an awful hurry to pour forth their thoughts and give cues that they expect those with whom they interact to keep pace. Two, "because of problems of reading."

The American accent could be a third barrier. On the one hand, students may face initial difficulties when they try to comprehend the accent. On the other hand, Americans who are seldom exposed to other English accents may be easily perplexed by a different accent or by a different stress put on a word. I have come into close contact with English spoken in its glorious and jarring variations by several ethnic groups in Singapore. This extended exposure to linguistic differences helps me appreciate some of the variations. Social anthropologist Marvin Mayers notes that the American has grown up in a "one-culture" world: "Frequently he enters high school or even college before becoming aware of dialectal differences in the English language. Instead of accepting and working with the differences he does encounter, all too often he has learned the monocultural ethnocentric approach of ridicule and mockery which tells the speaker with the 'accent' that he is an oddball, an outsider, and thus rejected."[6]

Edward Hall, in *Beyond Culture,* offers another perspective to this language problem. He was asked to evaluate some of the English language tests being administered to foreigners preparing to come to the United States for various types of training. The theory was that the foreign trainees would need to speak, read and write English. They should thus be tested for English competency before embarking on a training program in the United States. It seemed logical. In practice, many of those who passed tests given overseas were unable to understand what was going on when placed in actual classes in the

United States. They could not communicate in English in even the most basic and simplest situation. Part of the problem lay in the fact that there is no such thing as a basic form of the language that is universally applicable. "During our studies, we concluded that people anywhere in the world master hundreds of what we came to call 'situational dialects' which are used in specific situational frames, none of which is the language taught in the classroom. More important, the classroom is the only place where the classroom form of the language will be found. It is a monument to the human intellect that it has been able to overcome the handicap of classroom instruction and move into the living language."[7] Ordering meals in restaurants or buying a railroad ticket are examples of situational dialects. Everything is condensed: grammar, vocabulary, intonation.

Remedial help in English is needed for most international students. Irwin Sanders and Jennifer Ward in *Bridges to Understanding* say, "Because of the lack of overseas facilities for screening and despite the development of the TOEFL examination, many institutions find that they must provide additional English language training for students who were supposed to have adequate ability."[8]

In the case of graduate students, Sanders and Ward observe that the Teaching of English as a Second Language (TESL) noncredit program greatly increased their grade-point average and capability for serving as graduate assistants. Also, the students' success in the TESL program was related to previous familiarity with English.

International students' proficiency in English is of crucial importance to their welfare in the United States. Besides their academic performance, their social intercourse depends on their linguistic ability to make themselves easily understood in English. Spaulding and Flack conclude that international students with inadequate oral or written English language skills tended to run into both academic and social adjustment problems.[9] Facility with English is also found to be related to social and emotional adjustment.[10]

Here, then, is a vast area of international student need that an American could attempt to meet.

A Conflict of Educational Philosophies

Many international students come from cultures that give deference to teachers. Such an educational environment is in sharp conflict with an average American university. In their own countries the students tend to accept the teacher's word as absolute. They are discouraged from questioning data presented by the teacher. They also tend to learn by rote because examinations are often designed to reward those who can regurgitate data. Original ideas and thinking are either discouraged or must have the prior approval of the teacher before they can be presented in written form. Otherwise the students will be penalized for "wrong" ideas. The students' fear of embarrassment should they give a "wrong" answer also inhibits their verbal participation in the classroom.

Such an educational philosophy and cultural background place these students at an initial disadvantage in the American educational setting in two ways. First, their previous experiences have not prepared them for the American classroom. They are bewildered by what seems to them an American idiosyncrasy: students may freely interrupt a professor during a lecture. They may wish to add a stray thought to the professor's presentation, ask him to elaborate, or challenge him. It took me many months to feel comfortable with this practice by students of interjecting a professor's lecture with worldly wisdom.

Second, these students fumble over assignments that require interpretation or integration of concepts. James Plueddemann, former dean of Wheaton College Graduate School, aware of this contrasting educational philosophy, recounts a pertinent incident.[11] He gave an objective test in the first half of a course. Reflection-integration papers were assigned for the second half. During the latter period, one of the international students in his class asked, "Can I do an objective test instead of a reflection paper?"

"Why?" asked Professor Plueddemann.

She replied, "Because I want to get the right answer."

"I don't want you to get *the* right answer. I don't think there is *the* right answer. I want you to struggle with ideas."

"My educational system hasn't encouraged me to struggle with ideas, but to get the right answer. And I don't know what the right answer is. What if you don't like my ideas or philosophy?"

"Your goal is not to guess what my philosophy is. Your goal is to figure out for yourself what a good philosophy would be."

"But how do I know if I would get a good grade?"

"If you struggle very hard and show me that you are trying to integrate a philosophy with all parts of the Bible and the readings we've had in education, you'll get an A."

"But how do I know what you're looking for?"

"I'm not looking for any particular thing. I'm looking for an indication that you are struggling with ideas."

The international student's difficulty, observes Plueddemann, is the result of a cultural expectation of education. He elaborates, "It has to do with cultural values that encourage a student to want either to please the teacher or to get the right answer. And some cultural values do make it difficult for a person to wrestle impersonally with ideas."

Given time, most international students can adapt satisfactorily to the American educational system. Encouragement from a professor to make the transition facilitates change. Other variables could expedite the process. I do not, for instance, face difficulty with reflection-integration papers. My experience in courtmartial work as a lieutenant in the army and editorial writing as a magazine editor equips me for such papers. On the other hand, I dislike multiple-choice examinations. They are virtually confined to elementary school in the educational system I grew up in.

Getting to Know You

Students from the same country or ethnic group tend to form

close-knit subcultural clusters on the campus. Most of the students' social needs are met within these somewhat ethnically exclusive cliques. Immersed in their own cultural circle, they appear self-sufficient. They don't seem to need American friends or wish to know about the American way of life. This is often more apparent than real.

A non-Christian student from China says that he attends an American Bible study group because he wishes "to learn something of the customs and religion of Americans."[12] Yi-Qiang Xiong, an associate professor in Beijing Agriculture University before coming to the United States for doctoral studies in grain science, is not exceptional in this sentiment. He has his own group of more than twenty students from China on campus. Nonetheless he accepted the invitation to attend the Bible study because he perceives that there are Americans interested in him and his welfare. It is the exceptional student who wants to have nothing to do with his or her host country or its people after traveling thousands of miles to the United States. However, negative experiences with Americans could result in withdrawal symptoms.

One facet of American customs and religion has to do with Thanksgiving and Christmas. An invitation to spend these occasions in an American home is warmly anticipated by most international students. A home is a symbol of warmth, belonging, acceptance. Its informal atmosphere creates an environment conducive to interpersonal communication at a more meaningful level than the superficial exchanges that can characterize conversations carried out under the pressure of daily schedules.

International students have social needs that are partly met within their ethnic circle. They also have needs which can only be met by their American hosts.

Talents Ready for the Harvest

Four months after I arrived in the United States, the news editor of *Christianity Today* magazine phoned me. One of his editorial assistants was going on vacation. Could I help him part-time? I continued to appreciate Harry Genet's confidence in me and have enjoyed working with him both at Christianity Today, Inc. and later at World Evangelical Fellowship, editing *Global Report*.

Since writing is my major talent, I readily appreciated James Reapsome's offer in the spring of 1982 to write an article on Singapore for the *Evangelical Missions Quarterly*. I have also received much practical support from other editors since then.

Most graduate international students come from diverse backgrounds and experiences. They have talents ready to be harvested by those who seek them out. Christian international students are often willing to be resource persons at missions conferences. I wrote a brief report on one such conference for *Leadership 100* magazine:

Watching slides of Nigeria is one thing. Talking to a real-life Nigerian in your living room is something else.

That's why for the past three Novembers First Presbyterian Church in Deerfield, Illinois, has spiced its mission conference with foreign students. After getting names from nearby Christian colleges and seminaries, "we send personalized invitations to come and be our guests in our homes for the weekend," says Pastor Bernard F. Didier.

Members gladly welcome the internationals, finding out about their countries and also discussing the presentations at church by the conference's career missionary speakers.

Side benefits include:

Students with musical talents or slides of their countries are scheduled into the program.

Students are given a few minutes at the two Sunday morning services to share their plans as well as prayer concerns for their countries.

Students get to interact with each other. "The interplay among the participants," says Didier, "is as important as any one feature."

Bonds of friendship are established that often result in the students being invited back to the church.[13]

I mentioned the talents Christian internationals already have to Nate Mirza (who serves on the executive committee of the Association of Christian Ministries to Internationals). He made this suggestion: the school should compile a list of names of students with their curriculum vitae and mail it to ACMI so that it could circulate the list among churches interested in recruiting international students for their programs.

This excellent suggestion is based on the assumption that American church leaders would take the initiative of inviting International students to participate in their activities. It is an initiative that carries the element of crosscultural risk. An American knows the social conventions. A five-minute testimony means five minutes. An international student may not be so time-conscious. But the value of hearing firsthand from international students usually far outweighs the risks.

Keeping Up with the Joneses

I met Dave and Nicky Jones a few days after my arrival in the United States. We were out jogging on a warm late-summer evening. Dave, a newly arrived graduate student, immediately invited me to dinner. It was the beginning of a friendship that continues to unite us although we are now on different continents.

Dave and Nicky are now missionaries in Italy, but they were engaged in crosscultural activities long before they left the North American continent. They constantly went out of their way to befriend international students and to include them in their social and recreational activities. This meant going far beyond the perfunctory, "Hi! How are you?" It took them, for instance, half an hour to invite a Korean student and his family to join them for a swim. At the end of their elaborate explanation, they were still not too sure if their invitation was comprehended. The Korean's inability to converse in English would have turned off many people, American or otherwise. It worked the other way too. He would hesitate to initiate a conversation in English.

An attitude of acceptance was the foundation on which the Joneses built their relationships with international students. No ethnocentric specter marred our friendship. They did not indicate that I should conform to American standards and thus obviated any rejection should I fail to do so. Their attitude fostered togetherness. We shared our experiences, thoughts and lives as we met once a week in their home.

Sharing flowed over into other areas. It was in their Toyota that I learned to switch from a right-hand to a left-hand-drive car. Dave and Nicky also taught their two daughters not to keep their toys to themselves. They were to allow the children of international students to play with them. It was a lesson well learned. When Dave graduated and they were preparing to leave campus, Nicky wanted to sell some of the toys. Six-year-old Rebecca was upset. Sell? They should be given free to their international friends. "She made me feel so mercenary," Nicky said.

An overwhelming sense of acceptance and welcome by Americans through their actions is an international student need which Dave and Nicky fulfilled. They are certainly a couple of Joneses worth keeping up with.

CHAPTER 3

OVERCOMING
CULTURAL BARRIERS

MY WIFE AND I WALKED HESITANTLY INTO THE UNIVERSITY OF
Wisconsin's Union House to keep an appointment with an
Iranian. Although we were meeting for the first time, he spotted
us before we took more than a dozen steps past the entrance,
approached us and warmly welcomed us. Within the minute, as
we stood talking, he excused himself and went off with one of
his friends. Pam and I gazed briefly around the bustling
concourse before he returned.

Our Middle-Eastern friend was a popular figure. I soon had
his full attention as we sat down in the cafeteria to talk. That,
however, did not prevent his eyes from roaming the cafeteria.
He would nod, smile, wave at friends passing by. Once he
abruptly stood up, stopped himself in midsentence and, without
a word, left us so he could talk to one of his friends. When he
resumed his seat, I said I was comfortable with his mannerisms,
but that if I were an American who judged him by American
standards of communication, I might feel offended with his

behavior. His immediate response was that we need to establish "ground rules" with Americans from the start to avoid misunderstanding.

In this chapter I will attempt to discuss some areas where ground rules are helpful if communication between cultures is to flow smoothly.

Judging an Ethnic Group by Its Stereotypes

It amuses me when the Chinese are described as "inscrutable" or the East as "exotic." I am a Chinese but do not consider myself any more inscrutable than an American regards himself to be inscrutable. I have traveled in Southeast Asia but do not consider it any more exotic than the United States, England or Scotland. What is exotic in Western eyes is commonplace to me. The reverse is also true.

I am, nevertheless, as much in bondage to or freed from stereotypes as the next person. Thinking in stereotypes was more overt in my younger days. My elementary school peers and I referred to all Whites as "red-haired devils" or "red-faced monkeys."

The tendency to think in national or ethnic stereotypes is not confined to any one nation or ethnic group. In stereotyping, members of one nation or ethnic group see members of another in preconceived attitudes and beliefs. Stereotypes may undergo metamorphic, Jekyll-Hyde changes. One case involved the Chinese on the West Coast of the United States in the last century.[1] Newspapers and journals used positive stereotypes of the Chinese—"the most worthy of our newly adopted citizens," "the best immigrants in California," "adaptability beyond praise"—when the Chinese were needed in the West. They were extolled over the influx of White workers because the White labor force had no patience with domestic or factory work that the Chinese were engaged in. The Whites were too anxious to get rich quickly.

This flattering image of the thrifty, sober, inoffensive Chinese vanished when the glowing economic climate lost its

California suntan. The recession led other groups to compete
with the Chinese for their positions. In the electioneering
rhetoric of 1867 both political parties waxed eloquent over the
need for legislation to protect Californians against "Mongoli-
an" competition. The Chinese were castigated as clannish,
servile, deceitful. They smuggled opium, were undesirable as
workers and residents, and Chinatowns spawned prostitution
and gambling dens. It wasn't that the Chinese changed; the
economic situation did. Negative stereotypes were a repercus-
sion.

Christians are just as likely to apply stereotypes or labels. An
experiment by Gregory Razran showed that stereotypes may
actually affect the Christian's perception of people in an ethnic
group.[2]

Thirty out of several thousands of photographs of college
girls were selected from the undergraduate yearbooks of
Stanford University, Wisconsin University and Swarthmore
College. The selection was based on a facial type that was
ethnically nonspecific and could fit most American White
groupings. Each photograph would not arouse doubt or
suspicion if a typically Jewish, Italian or Irish surname were
attached to it. A second criterion was good looks. Both criteria
were met. Three groups of fifty people (two groups were college
students) were shown the thirty photographs projected one at
a time, life-size, on a screen and asked to judge on a one-to-
five scale for general liking, beauty, intelligence, character,
ambition and ability to entertain.

Two months later these three groups were again shown the
original thirty photographs and asked to rate them. On this
occasion, surnames were attached to all the photographs. Five
had Jewish surnames such as Rabinowitz, Kantor; five Italian
surnames such as Fichetti, LaGuardia; five Irish surnames such
as McGillicuddy, O'Brien; and fifteen old American surnames
such as Adams, Chase.

The results showed that those with Jewish and Italian
surnames had a significant drop in ratings for general liking,

and a smaller drop for beauty and character. Ambition ratings, however, were raised, especially for those with Jewish surnames. Mere labeling of the photographs with ethnic surnames affected the responses.

The religious affiliation of each of the three groups was: thirty-three Protestants, fourteen Catholics, one Greek Orthodox and two Jewish.

Another problem with national stereotypes is that they respect no boundaries. I have noticed that the attitudes of a Chinese elder in a Plymouth Brethren church in Singapore are amazingly similar to that of his American counterpart in the United States. The values of a middle-class church in Singapore and the United States also have marked similarities.

Each cultural group's composition is often too complex to be reduced to one homogeneous list of characteristics. But television, the theater, the press, books, idioms and superficial contact with foreigners contribute to the formation of stereotypes. Although sometimes arbitrary, stereotypes need not be totally groundless. Cultural differences do exist. The difficulty lies in formulating them.

Stereotyping, moreover, feeds a judgmental attitude. We form opinions of individuals and groups without adequate data. Hitler, in *Mein Kampf,* wrote only of the Jewish race, not of the individual Jew. It is far easier to construct a stereotype and annihilate it than to destroy individuals we know.

Communication is hindered in stereotyping. If a person thinks that Italians and Jews are obnoxious people, then he or she notices only those actions which reinforce the preconceived label. This selective perception seems to do justice to a judgmental attitude. In reality it drags a person deeper into the mire of pride and prejudice. Crosscultural communication is facilitated if we relate to one another on an individual basis.

The Boss in the Classroom
Most Asian cultures require students to be very deferential to authority if they wish to succeed in school. As students in

Teachers' Training College, Singapore, my friends and I agreed that the vast majority of our instructors, including one who had a Ph.D. from the United States, were paradigms of how not to teach. Yet none of us formally complained. We were excessively docile. Good instructors were a bonus. Bad instructors were tolerated. Attendance was taken, and if it had been Sunday school we would have made the honor roll. The instructor was master of all he surveyed, at least in the classroom. Rumor had it that he kept a little black book. If a student aroused his ire, his name was etched into it, and his final grades would be lowered.

A proper distance was also maintained between instructor and student. We would have committed a serious breach of conduct if we addressed an instructor by his first name even if he were only a few years our senior. Evaluation of an instructor's performance or the relevancy of a course by students was an unheard-of phenomenon.

If the situation in Singapore is non-American, that in Japan is even more so. Professor Stephen Franklin was accorded enormous status by his students and his Japanese neighbors during his five years as a professor in a Japanese university.[3] He had a very high ranking on the vertical Japanese societal hierarchy. Besides his professional status, Franklin functioned as a lowly student when he was learning the Japanese language. In the Japanese context, a teacher expects a large measure of gratitude and lifelong indebtedness from his students. The teacher is the master and the student acknowledges this through his verbal and nonverbal behavior, especially that of adopting the correct postures in the teacher's presence. He did very well with most of his Japanese teachers. As a foreigner he was usually excused from such social demands. "But," he says, "there would be some of them who would treat me the way I feel a twelve-year-old should be treated instead of a person in his middle thirties because of the teacher-student relationship."

Summing up he says, "On the one hand, when I functioned as a professor, it probably put me too high from where I should have been from an American point of view. On the other hand, when I functioned as a student, I was occasionally treated in a way that, were I in America, I would have construed it an insult to my dignity as a person. I don't want to say that I didn't enjoy my experience in Japan or that I wouldn't go back. I would. But I never got used to functioning in a hierarchical society in such a dissonance of social roles."

The Newcomer Has to Take the Initiative
An increasing sense of guilt burdened me soon after I completed a year of studies in the United States. It had to do with the stewardship of my talents and my sense of belonging to my college.

The student-produced weekly newspaper seemed amateurish. And there I was with my journalistic experience and not helping. I had my excuses. I was carrying an academic overload of twenty hours. I was serving on the International Student Fellowship committee on campus. As ex-editor I was contributing book reviews to my magazine in Singapore. Busy or otherwise, I could not dislodge my burden. There was only one route to take: volunteer my services.

I first established contact through a telephone call. Then one moonlit night in late summer I went to the newspaper office to talk to the editor, a senior. I was politely received.

I told him of my qualifications. Besides writing for Singapore publications, I had written articles for a national Episcopal newspaper in Australia and *Christianity Today* magazine.

"Wow!" he said, shaking his head in mild wonder. Or so I thought. "I can do with your help."

The dialog was proceeding along the right direction. "I'll be graduating in December," I said.

"Oh." He sounded disappointed.

"But I'll be around in grad school here and would continue to help."

"That's good. I was hoping you would."

I returned to my apartment with a much lighter conscience.

Soon after, the news editor assigned me an article on a blood drive. She said the Aurora Area Blood Bank would be on campus and the article was to create some awareness of the need to donate blood. When the story was published I was unhappy with the editing, but decided it was premature to present my critique. That, as it turned out, was my first and last contribution. I was not asked to write a second article.

This is a situation fraught with variables. Several hypotheses could be pursued. A pertinent one has to do with cultural differences. A key question is, Who takes the initiative when an acknowledged leader meets a newcomer?

In my Christian community in Singapore the initiative lies almost exclusively with those in authority. A year after I accepted Christ as Savior at age twenty-one, I was asked if I would be a Sunday-school teacher. Two years later I was asked to consider being a deacon. Such invitations are carried out on a person-to-person basis. Pulpit announcements just do not work. If someone is perceived to be capable, no is an answer that is not automatically accepted. In a sense it is an initiation rite. Newcomers are not expected to say yes to a first invitation. If they are worthy of a first invitation, they are worthy of repeated invitations. As a leader in my church, I was similarly sensitive to members with leadership potential. New members would be gently probed for their interests, talents, past service. It is the business of leaders to know their members.

On the other hand, newcomers who volunteer too eagerly for leadership positions are eyed with suspicion. It could be a sign of swaggering self-confidence, egotistical individuality, pride. Modesty and humility are the preferred marks of newcomers. Even when asked they do not rattle off their resumé. Before coming to the United States I met an American who did just that in a matter-of-fact fashion. I was struck by his nonchalance. I must admit that I have since on occasion done the same thing with Americans.

In the American Christian society that I am acquainted with, I often perceive that newcomers have to take the initiative. And they must keep at it until they have established themselves. The community does not offer them a place.

Time, Tide and the Wedding Dinner

Time and tide, it is said, waits for no man. Not even on his wedding day.

The traditional Chinese believes that significant events, like weddings, should be held on auspicious days. One such day on the Chinese calendar fell on a Saturday. Six of my friends decided to marry on the same day. The solemnization of their marriages was held in church at staggered times: 11 A.M., 2 P.M., 3:30 P.M. It was a December day during the monsoon period and the rains fell. And fell. And fell. Parts of Singapore were flooded by midafternoon. The floods were aggravated by high tide in the evening. Roads were either impassable or were badly snarled by Saturday night traffic.

One couple, Stanley and Christine, held their wedding dinner at a posh restaurant. It was to start at "7:30 P.M. sharp." At least that was the time on the invitation card. Tradition, however, told me not to expect food to be served until about 8:45 P.M. As it turned out, it was 10:15 P.M. before the feasting began. It was the typical ten-course Chinese dinner to be eaten at a leisurely pace. The couple's parents felt that many of their guests would be delayed. They did not wish to begin dinner until most of them had arrived. As for me, I had left home at 6:30 P.M. to accommodate the crawling traffic and detours for the ten-mile drive. My watch welcomed Sunday morning as I was driving home from the dinner.

Punctuality is important in Singapore. It is the second busiest port in the world. Its international airport is one of the most efficient in Asia. It is also a financial and banking center. We are time-oriented. This time consciousness, however, gives way at the traditional Chinese wedding dinner. It has social conventions of its own. Knowing this helps us adjust our stomach clocks accordingly.

Conflicts may arise when a time-oriented person meets a

nontime-oriented or event-oriented person. Americans over-emphasize being on time. Professor Taussig says, "An American invites his international friend for dinner, and the international comes an hour late. The American says to him, 'Why are you late?' And the international replies, 'Well, I'm here.' The American says, 'But you are late.' A lack of understanding of this cultural matter causes misunderstanding and has even broken some friendships."[4]

Mayers identifies twelve categories of basic values, including that of time.[5] These descriptive categories attempt to objectify a culture without placing a value judgment on it. He distinguished time-oriented persons from event-oriented persons. As implied, the former are concerned with the time period. It is of a certain length depending on the intent or purpose of the time to be spent. They are also concerned with the range of punctuality at the beginning and end of the time period. They carefully plan to accomplish the most possible in the time allotted. They set goals—long, middle and short range—which are related to a time period, whether it be hours, days, weeks, months or years. They attempt to condense into a given period as much as they can of that which they consider worthwhile. There is likely to be a time/dollar equivalence, or a time-spent/production equivalence in their way of life. If they spend a certain number of hours studying for a test, they expect a certain grade. They remember and try to reinforce certain times and dates.

On the other hand, event-oriented people are not too concerned with the time period. They bring people together without planning a detailed schedule. They work over a problem or idea until it is resolved or exhausted, regardless of time. They live in the here-and-now and do not have a detailed plan for the future. Rather than rely on the experience of others, they trust their own experience implicitly. They have little empathy with, and confidence in, the experience of others unless it is communicated to them through some form of sharing.

My Values Are Not Your Values

A month after my article "Why Foreign Students Usually Hate the United States" was published, I received a letter from an African.[6] He wanted me to sponsor him for studies in Wheaton College, Illinois. He wrote that he would wholeheartedly accept my sponsorship regardless of the obligations I might attach to it. He promised he would not disappoint me.

I failed to understand him as I viewed him from my background. I am wary of financial sponsorships that have fine print attached to them. I will not accept a sponsorship unless I am confident of fulfilling the requirements or have them appropriately amended. I felt that the African, a stranger, was either foolhardy or believed that I am a Christian and therefore a benign person who would not make unreasonable demands on him.

Much later I gained an insight into his values. James Plueddemann explains: "If an African was writing to you and asking, 'Would you sponsor me?' it could have been looked at from *his* point of view. He could be saying, 'I will be your follower. And if you have a lot of followers, it will help you move up. So I will hang on to your coattails, but I will also push. And when you move forward, I'll move forward too.' "[7] Looked at from this standpoint, I could appreciate the African's thoughts, his sense of dignity and his concept of community or teamwork.

In *Christianity Confronts Culture*, Mayers states that every social group, subculture or community has its own pattern or network of values. These values are what make a community unique. They cause a community to grow and maintain interest in life. Without them life would become ordinary and hum-drum. A given community may have values that are distinct from those of some other society, but there is no real difficulty in finding values within every society or subculture. Sometimes an outsider feels that a given society *should* have other values than those they do have, but this is because of an extreme focus on his or her own way of life. These feelings are actually a negative expression of ethnocentrism.[8]

Warm and Cold Contexts

Americans who say, "Hi! How are you?" are seldom out to seek medical, social or psychological information from their friends. Nor are they necessarily conveying concern for their friends' welfare. It is usually nothing more than a casual greeting. For instance, two people walking in opposite directions may not even pause in their stride during their exchange of civilities. An international student unaware of this social convention may be initially put off by such behavior. One annoyed Indonesian graduate student said, "He asked 'How are you?' and then walked away before I could tell him how I was feeling!" This almost impersonal practice was mistaken for a warm greeting, a cue to stand around and chat.

Communication across cultural boundaries may be hindered by a failure to perceive behavior in context. Hall refers to two contexts: high and low.[9]

High-context behavior is warm, intimate, involved, friendly. The high-context person communicates with more than just the exact meaning of words. He or she communicates with hands, eyes, tone of voice. Allowance is made for considerable bending of the system in such a culture because the bonds between people are strong.

Low-context behavior, on the other hand, is official, status-conscious, ceremonial. The low-context person communicates almost entirely through the use of exact words. In the low-context culture the bonds that tie people together are somewhat fragile. People move away or withdraw if things are not going well. It takes a long time for such a person to become deeply involved with others, and for some this never occurs.

Tensions arise when a person from a high-context country, such as Africa, comes to a low-context American institution. Professor Plueddemann says, "I had one African student come to me, weeping, saying, 'Look, I came to see you. How many times? I came to visit you in your office. I came to visit you in

your home. We had you over for a meal. Then you give me a
B minus. And I worked very hard.' "

Professor Plueddemann tried to explain: " 'It doesn't mean
that if you work one hundred hours you get an A, and if you
work ninety hours you get a B. It's not how many hours you
work and how many times you come to see me. It's how you
do on the test.'

" 'Oh,' he said, 'but that's very cold, impersonal and unchris-
tian.' "

Rules are spelled out clearly in a low-context American
institution. The syllabi and catalog function almost as legal
contracts. The reaction of a high-context student is, "Why do
you have so many rules for international students?" or "Now
that you know me, get rid of the rules." Says Plueddemann, "For
an African student to go and get an apartment and be told, 'You
have to pay two months rent now' is an affront to him. His
reaction is, 'Don't you trust *me*? You don't trust *Africans*?' "[10]

Misunderstanding undermines healthy interpersonal relationships. An understanding of other cultures alerts us to the
communication of unintended meanings.

PART 2:

SHARING THE GOOD NEWS

CHAPTER 4

THE CRUCIAL CONTACT

I WAS APPALLED BY A PARACHURCH ORGANIZATION WHICH SEIZED the opportunity during orientation and registration to conduct an "evangelistic blitz" on campus. I felt that such a hasty, large-scale, aggressive effort was a sign of insensitivity. The theoretical objective was to obey the Great Commission by reaching out in love to the new students. It also appeared to be an attempt to steal the initiative from other Christian campus groups. The mandate to preach the gospel seemed to be issued by a demanding human boss concerned for statistics rather than given by a loving God.

One of my Christian friends, then a freshman, said she was confronted seven times on campus by members of this group with their canned version of the gospel. She said she must have "a pagan-looking face."

This breathless rush both to establish a beachhead and to confront new students with an inflexible version of the gospel was often done without any attempt to relate it to the students' needs. If we wish to be effective we should not concentrate solely on the spiritual while ignoring the practical, social and academic needs.

Effective evangelism is seldom easy. Crosscultural evangelism is even more difficult. Thom Hopler, who spent ten years as a missionary in Kenya, says it was not hard for him to stay in the mission station and fellowship with other American missionaries. It was the comfortable thing to do. "I had to force myself to get out of the mission station and down into the village to deal with people who spoke an unfamiliar language, ate unfamiliar food, held unfamiliar values and functioned in an unfamiliar culture," says Hopler. "It was difficult to communicate the gospel in that setting."[1]

Hopler's candid admission is insightful. Crosscultural work begins with a decision to embark on such a mission. Unlike Hopler, Americans living in the vicinity of a campus with international students do not have to travel far. As their cost of commitment is much cheaper than Hopler's, they have to guard against a temptation to abandon a commitment to minister to the students.

It takes discipline of mind and spirit to forsake the comforts of the familiar for the rigors of the unfamiliar. Hopler had to do this to establish direct, personal contact with the Africans. The chasm between the decision to act and the actual process of doing is just as difficult for other Americans to bridge. They form the majority ethnic group and are in the comfortable confines of their home ground.

This chapter emphasizes establishing and maintaining contact.

Welcome to My World
Twenty-nine hours after leaving Singapore I landed at O'Hare Airport, Chicago, just before 6 A.M. It was Labor Day, 1980. A thundershower shrouded the glow of dawn. One thought was uppermost in my mind: would anyone from my college meet me at the airport? The late arrival of Form I-20 from my college

had delayed my student visa application. I had sent a telegram to the college informing it of my flight arrangements the moment the visa was cleared, barely two days before I left my country.

With the help of overhead signs, I arrived at the baggage claim area. Some of these porters have a way of making your fears come true, I thought, when I noticed that a wheel was missing from one of my suitcases. I placed my hand luggage next to my suitcases and gazed expectantly at the faces around me. The baggage claim area soon grew deserted. I gave up hope. I decided to pack my Bible into my suitcase.

As I was doing so, an American voice sounded over me: "Are you Lawson Lau?" Bill Hill, associate dean of student development of Wheaton College Graduate School, mispronounced my last name. Nevertheless, they were the most welcome words I'd heard since I left home.

Many hands made light work of lugging my two suitcases, a hand bag, a coat and a camera. They quickly disappeared into the trunk of his Honda Accord. I had expected to be away from home for five years and was not traveling light. We soon drove out from under the protection of the terminal into the downpour. The distant sound of rumbling thunder which accompanied the occasional flash of lightning was no gun salute. But it no longer depressed my spirits. There shall be showers of blessing, I thought. It was great to be alive. I was in the competent hands of none other than a native of the United States of America.

My parents were very moved when I wrote to tell them that a Bill Hill from my school took the trouble to meet me at the airport on a rainy morning during a national holiday. An act beyond the call of duty, they felt. Bill was on a weekend retreat and returned on Sunday to get the message that I was arriving the next morning.

Since then I have welcomed other international students at the airport. And I know of many Americans and veteran international students who have done so. The Foreign Student

Office on campus usually has details of incoming students'
flight arrangements. Its full-time staff are often happy to have
the help of volunteers, especially at peak periods in their
calendar.

Welcoming international students weighed down with luggage at the air, bus or train terminal is an ideal start to a crosscultural relationship. It establishes contact at a vital point in the
student's sojourn in the United States. Showing such a concern
for the student tends to crumble barriers between people of different cultures. It also meets a need.

A Spectrum of Needs

International students have a wide spectrum of pressing needs
during their initial weeks on campus. Among the major ones
are finding suitable housing, knowing which type of bank account to open, shopping for food and clothes, overcoming loneliness, and understanding the American educational system.

Psychologist Abraham Maslow identifies five categories of
needs.[2] At the base of his hierarchy of needs are physiological needs such as hunger. If these are relatively well gratified,
safety needs will surface. Here people look for structure, order,
law and limits, security, and freedom from fear, anxiety and
chaos.

If the physiological and safety needs are fairly well met,
needs for love and affection and belongingness will emerge.
At this level people keenly feel the absence of friends, or
sweethearts, or spouses or family. They hunger for affectionate
relations with people in general and strive to achieve such
relationships. They may even forget that once, when they were
hungry, they sneered at love as unreal, unnecessary or unimpor-
tant. Now they feel sharply the pangs of loneliness, ostracism,
rejection, friendlessness, rootlessness.

Next are esteem needs. Maslow classifies them into two
subsidiary sets. First is the desire for strength, achievement,
adequacy, mastery and competence, confidence in the face of
the world, and independence and freedom. Second is the

desire for reputation or prestige (defined as respect or esteem
from other people), status, fame and glory, dominance,
recognition, dignity or appreciation. Satisfaction of these leads
to feelings of self-confidence, worth, strength, and being useful
and necessary. Thwarting these needs, however, produces
feelings of inferiority, weakness and helplessness.

Self-actualization needs top the hierarchy. Maslow contends
that even if all the preceding needs are satisfied, a new
discontent and restlessness will soon develop unless people are
doing what they are fitted for. They must be true to their own
nature. The specific form that the self-actualization needs take
will consequently vary from person to person.

Maslow maintains that people lacking food, safety, love and
esteem would probably hunger for food more strongly than for
anything else. The lower levels of needs have to be fairly well
satisfied before they are motivated to seek for the gratification
of needs higher on the hierarchy.

A weakness in Maslow's hierarchy is the lack of any
consideration of spiritual needs. Nevertheless it reminds us of
a student's needs. A student anxious about obtaining housing
is unlikely to appreciate a discourse on the wise man who built
his house upon a rock. Practical help is his immediate need.
James points out: "If a brother or sister is ill-clad and in lack
of daily food, and one of you says to them, 'Go in peace, be
warmed and filled,' without giving them the things needed for
the body, what does it profit? So faith by itself, if it has no works,
is dead" (Jas 2:15-17).

Jesus is sensitive to both our practical and spiritual needs. His
striking claim at the start of his ministry is: "The Spirit of the
Lord is upon me, because he has anointed me to preach good
news to the poor. He has sent me to proclaim release to the
captives and recovering of sight to the blind, to set at liberty
those who are oppressed, to proclaim the acceptable year of the
Lord" (Lk 4:18-19). Jesus fulfilled what he came into the world
to do, namely, to meet our physical, emotional, psychological
and spiritual needs. Christ's example is our foundation for

ministering to others, including international students.

Friendships That Blossom

This emphasis on establishing early contact with international students is based on several considerations. Professor Taussig says, "A very important aspect of our ministry to international students is that the student finds an American friend who will serve and love him as soon as he arrives on the campus. His needs are greatest at this point. A lot of effort has to be put into finding Americans who are willing to adopt as friend a newly-arrived international student so that he can help to get him oriented to our culture. The American can take his international friend shopping, show him around the town, and instruct him in banking and the registration and educational processes that he will soon be involved in."[3]

He stresses that "the best relationships we've seen in our whole program are relationships that were started the day the international student arrived in Manhattan. An American friend would help him immediately. These friendships seem to last throughout the student's entire stay."

Such an approach to friendship contains viable seeds that hold out the promise of relationships that will grow and blossom.

"On the other hand," adds Taussig, "if we waited until the international student has been here on our campus for some months, then the friendship relationship is much more difficult to etablish because the student already has a certain measure of orientation. He has found friends from his own culture and is busy with his studies. To start a friendship after the international student has been here for some time is not nearly as easy nor as needy as on his arrival."

Two more points. First, most Americans find it daunting to talk to foreigners. Once international students are absorbed into a subcultural or national group on campus, the barrier becomes even more formidable and forbidding. They no longer appear to have a gnawing need for American friendships or for an orientation to American culture. They are usually less responsive to belated overtures of friendship.

Academic pressure is the other factor. The American educational system soon besieges students with assignments and papers. International students are often very conscious of their academic obligations and objectives. They have traveled thousands of miles to the United States. Tuition is expensive and is made more so by the currency exchange rate. Their parents, relatives and friends back home expect them to perform a nice series of academic miracles. The pressure to obtain good grades may exert an almost oppressive hold over them. Sociologist William Liu says, "In the Confucian ethic, which permeates the cultures of China, Japan, Viet Nam and Korea, scholastic achievement is the only way of repaying the infinite debt to parents, of showing filial piety."[4] This may mean that if friendships have not been formed prior to the onset of academic pressure, the students are less likely to respond at a later time to social invitations that will draw them away from their books.

Small Talk That Impedes Growth
Pam and I usually phone home several times a year. These international calls are reserved for special occasions—Christmas, Mom's birthday, Chinese New Year. Such calls are kept short, as it is expensive to reach out and touch someone on another continent. It is always a thrill to hear the familiar, unique voice of each family member. Before each call we draw up a list of items to update family members about events since our last letter home. Once the greetings are over and these brief items are mentioned, a problem arises. What shall we say then? Pauses punctuate the conversation. Time constraints often restrain us from launching into a fresh subject or doing any in-depth sharing. Our conversation hovers around the conventional and trivial.

Although time constraints are not always present, conversing with a stranger or an acquaintance is far more awkward. Paul

Tournier, a physician and psychologist, says, "Think of what goes to make up most conversations: the exchange of superficial impressions ('What gorgeous weather!'); conventional remarks that do not always come from the heart ('How are you?'); observations whose true intention is self-justification or more or less cleverly to make the most of oneself; flattery; straightforward or veiled criticism."[5]

Tournier hastens to add that it would not be human to wish to divest conversation of everything superfluous. The small talk of everyday life does give some semblance of gracious living to the routine of daily life. More important, small talk can pave the road to getting to know the other person, a prelude to the meeting of two minds, of two hearts. But, he points out, small talk is too often used as a means of avoiding personal contact: "It allows us to be friendly and interesting with people without touching subjects that would compel us to enter into real dialogue."[6]

One irate Asian international student scolded an American student thus: "If you're not interested in how I am, don't ask me 'How are you?'!" She was angry over a thoughtless mind which happened not to be speechless.

While early contact with the international student is an excellent start to a relationship, it should be recognized for what it is—a beginning. Relationships are often fragile. Excessive small talk can inflict extensive damage. Friendships grow only if they are watered by concerns that delve below the surface of social conventions. For international students their studies, social life, work on campus, and home are some major branches on their tree of life. Conversation that enters into such areas of their lives waters the relationships. "Tell me about yourself (or your home, or your country)" usually elicits a good response. It is, however, irritating to be asked a question and, before the answer is given, to notice the look of utter boredom on the face of the inquirer. Genuine interest is vital.

A survey suggests that small talk could be a problem for the American college or university student. As many as 4,900

delegates at Inter-Varsity Christian Fellowship's missionary conference at Urbana, Illinois, responded to the survey. It listed
several problems in the personal evangelism section. The
problems were "no desire to witness, don't know how to start
conversations, can't explain the gospel, can't answer questions
about Christianity," and "I'm not sure it's all true." Of those
who listed problems, the large majority stated that they don't
know how to start conversations.

A researcher commented: "One could view this answer a
number of ways. It might be that they have a very limited view
of what it means to be a personal evangelist, emphasizing a
one-time verbal explanation of the gospel as opposed to seeing
evangelism as a continuous process. From the other side one
might conclude that they just need more training in how to
share their faith as a natural part of life. Or, again, this may
represent a more general problem with human relationships.
They may have difficulty starting any kind of conversation."[7]

This problem could be heightened in crosscultural evangelism. Solutions include a wholehearted interest in, a willingness
to spend time with, and a readiness to listen to an international
student.

Jesus' fellowship with the Samaritan woman is an outstand-
ing example of crosscultural witness. First, their meeting is not
accidental. He went out of his way to establish contact with her.
Then he had to overcome the prejudices of sex, race, religion
and the social consequences of initiating a conversation with
a woman of questionable repute. Moreover, from the woman's
perspective, Jesus was a Jew and therefore suspect. Jesus
surmounts these barriers to communication by starting the
conversation on a practical note. He says, "Give me a drink" (Jn
4:7). Jesus then uses this request to build rapport with the
woman.

A resurrected Christ also shows us how to enter into a
conversation by asking simple questions. He asks Cleopas and
his friend as they walked to Emmaus: "What is this conversation
which you are holding with each other as you walk?" (Lk 24:17).

Again, Jesus asks, "What things?" (v. 19). Cleopas and his companion were only too eager to share their knowledge with him.

Jesus has shown us how to start meaningful conversations. It could be creatively applied to situations with international students. The students are usually willing to impart their wealth of knowledge and experiences—if asked. Mutual sharing of knowledge and experiences makes for healthy relationships.

Mutual Respect Builds Relationships

Friendships or interpersonal relationships form in at least four ways. Social anthropologist Marvin Mayers discusses three points of view that develop only partial relationships: the traditionalist, the relativist and the adherents of situation ethics. He then develops the concept of mutual respect.[8]

Traditionalists see their world as one that never changes and should never change. They focus primarily on form or expression rather than meaning. The form should remain the same whatever the cost. A traditionalist who is a member of a traditional society would seek to perpetuate it. To get along with traditionalists, other people have to conform to them and must at least partially abandon their principles, beliefs and lifestyle.

People who perceive such an attitude in themselves need to be wary of it if they wish to be crosscultural workers. Such an outlook may feed a spirit of arrogance and lead to misunderstanding.

On the other hand, international students may adopt a traditionalistic attitude while in the United States. A Hong Kong couple, one of whom was a graduate student, decided they were not going to change. The American accent, values and lifestyle were not for them. They felt that any change while in the United States would render it more difficult for them to adjust back to the Hong Kong way of life when they returned. Their home church leaders and friends would also be critical of them if they absorbed any Americanisms.

Traditionalists fall on one end of the continuum. At the other

end are the relativists or antinomians. Relativists abandon all
that they are to cater or pander to other people. They forfeit
principle for the sake of others and may suffer a serious loss
of self-respect. They may become relativists by choice or
through the pressures of the society they are in.

Relativists are to be distinguished from cultural relativists.
The latter hold the view that truth can be expressed through
distinct cultural forms. Truth remains the same even though
the form may differ from culture to culture. Cultural relativists
encourage full maintenance of principle and responsibility.
Cultural relativism is a viable option for Christians.

Going native, a term I used earlier, also describes relativists.
Emotionally insecure or malleable international students are
likely to become relativists if they are besieged by ethnocentric
American peers. They may indiscriminately conform to them.
Relativists tend to prefer American companions and shun other
international students. Some American-born Chinese students,
for instance, take this route. A desire to project an urbane
image makes them avoid contact with their "uncouth" country
cousins from the undeveloped nations. They want to avoid
being embarrassed by their awkward, fumbling mannerisms.

In situation ethics a person may abandon a certain amount
of principle, whenever necessary, out of love for the other
person. "The situationist enters into every decision-making
situation fully armed with the ethical maxims of the community
and its heritage, and he treats them with respect as illuminators
of his problems. Just the same, he is prepared in any situation
to compromise them or set them aside in the situation if love
seems better served by doing so."[9]

This flexibility appears to be commendable. Mayers,
however, points out several problems with situation ethics.[10]
One practical problem is the potential for undermining trust.
This occurs in any decision involving other people. Though the
other people may initially like what has been done on their
behalf, they may later interpret the action differently. They may
view it as, to some degree, an abandonment of principle. This

change in perspective may disrupt or destroy relationships if the reinterpretation is not resolved.

Mutual respect, however, involves a balanced, reciprocal relationship. Each person perceives that his or her point of view is valid and worthy of being heard. Complete acceptance of one another, rather than prejudice, forms the basis of the relationship. Each person is permitted to realize fully his or her own potential. Neither has to abandon ethical or moral principles in an arbitrary fashion. Manipulation is absent in mutual respect. Non-Christians are not viewed as objects of evangelism. They are befriended as people created in the image of God and deserving of respect. In the crosscultural context mutual respect means that no culture is considered superior or more advanced than the other. Such respect also fosters trust. If trust is undermined, both parties will make every effort to restore the trust balance as the relationship is built on a foundation of two-way communication.

Compassion Is Two-Way Communication
Mutual respect fosters a spirit of compassion rather than mere sympathy. Sympathy could in fact hinder evangelism. Harvie Conn of Westminster Theological Seminary spent more than seven of his twelve years as a missionary in Korea doing evangelistic work with prostitutes. Two reasons motivated him to start this ministry. First, the prostitutes formed a sizable group of unreached people. Second, "I thought that they were rather clearly sinners," says Professor Conn. "I saw them as in rebellion against God and needing repentance. And I went calling them to faith. I defined their needs in terms of how I had seen needs in a North American pastorate."[11]

The fruits of his initial encounters were very few. The young women listened but never left prostitution. No one changed. The breakthrough came when one person began to change. Says Conn, "I changed."[12]

As he worked with the women, he gathered more information about the system of which they were a part. Many of them had entered prostitution because it was often the only work they could find in an Asian, male-dominated culture. The war had destroyed their links with the extended family system. They were often the senior breadwinners. There were brothers and sisters to take care of. Personal problems at home or a bad economic year sent the young women from rural homes to the big city to look for quick money. They were met at the trains by pimps who offered them a place to stay for the night. In the home they were gang-raped. When they got ready to leave, they were told that they had to pay for room and board. They couldn't, and found prostitution the only way to pay their debts. They had become slaves of a system from which they could not break free. Their humanity was buried in shame and guilt.

"I started suspecting my own early motivations," recalls Conn. "Was it sin I had really seen? Or the violation of middle-class morality? At this stage, my early sympathies seemed more like cultural morality."[13]

He became compassionate. A person is not just a sinner. He or she is also sinned against. "My cultural background in white, North American churches had oriented me almost exclusively to seeing a person as the subject of sin. But not the object of sin. Seeking the various factors that kept women in prostitution opened my eyes to that new dimension."[14]

Compassion is more than tenderness. It is tenderness translated into action on behalf of those sinned against. The Lord, for instance, said to Moses at the burning bush: "I have seen the affliction of my people who are in Egypt, and have heard their cry because of their taskmasters; I know their sufferings, and I have come down to deliver them" (Ex 3:7-8). The incarnation of Jesus Christ also demonstrates God's love and compassion for us. Compassion leads to identification, an entering into the experiences of another person with sensitivity and understanding.

Translated into action, compassion establishes two-way communication. Such communication surmounts barriers to friendship. Paul Little mentions two barriers. One is a patronizing manner. He says, "We must be careful not to give the impression to our foreign friends that we are just doing them a favor. They do not want us to do things *for* them but *with* them."[15]

Pride is the other. "Thinking of everything 'American' automatically as best and looking down on everything foreign is a common temptation. We must be willing to admit some deficiencies in our way of life and receive criticism graciously. At the same time, we must genuinely appreciate and respect accomplishments and cultures of other countries. We must not think that something different, like eating with chopsticks instead of knife and fork, is necessarily inferior. Nothing creates more resentment among internationals than our often unconscious superior attitude."[16]

Little's advice is important. Unhelpful attitudes are obstacles in a relationship. They result in one-way communication, a very ineffective way of conveying concern and care. Compassion builds bridges to friendships.

CHAPTER 5

PROCLAIMING THE GOSPEL

IT WAS A PLEASANT, UNSEASONABLY WARM WINTER DAY IN FEBRU-ary 1983 when I accompanied a friend to the airport. After helping him lug his suitcases to the airline's check-in counter, I walked rapidly through the concourse to his car parked outside the departure hall. When I neared the exit, a tidily dressed, clean-shaven, young American emerged from the crowd around me and partially obstructed my passage.

"Hello!" he greeted me in a loud voice.

"Hi!" I returned.

"Are you from China?" he shot back.

My curiosity was aroused. "No, Singapore."

"Are you new here?"

"No, I'm studying at Wheaton."

There seemed to be a fleeting moment of hesitation. He continued, "I have a book for you." He thrust a hardbound volume in my direction. By reflex I took it. "Could you come over to our counter for a minute?"

I glanced at the bright, full-color dust jacket. Two words caught my attention: "Hare Krishna." My curiosity was satiated. Ah! I thought, a cult strikes again. I hurried after him. The counter was about twenty feet away.

"Could I have your name and address?" he asked politely. "We'd like to visit with you."

"No, thank you," I replied. "I've got to go now."

I returned the book to one of several stacks of companion volumes on the counter. My last impression of the young man was a pen poised futilely over a notebook and a look of displeasure and annoyance on his face.

This incident reminded me of Christians who accost strangers with a bogus religious survey to present the gospel and elicit a decision for Christ. These strangers might have looked on us with as much suspicion as we would a member of a cult. Similarly, international students who are Buddhists or Hindus may not be anti-Christian. We may, however, provoke them to reject us and our gospel if they get the impression that our only interest in them is to convert them to Christianity. We seldom accommodate an aggressive cult devotee. International students may likewise dismiss us.

We are, moreover, dealing with neighbors on our campus, not strangers in a shopping mall. We have an extended time frame in which to interact with the non-Christian. It does not seem to warrant a less sensitive, hit-and-run method of evangelism. The authenticity of our lives has to match our proclamation.

Stepping Out on a Spiritual Journey

The journey of a thousand miles, so goes a Chinese proverb, begins with the first step. Our Christian duty may be conceived of as helping our friends, including non-Christians, to move onward in their spiritual journey. Walking alongside our friends part of the way is an effective route to take.

There are two striking dimensions of hundreds of testimonies that I have heard. One is their uniqueness. Patterns may be discerned, but exact circumstances are never duplicated. Zacchaeus, Paul, Cornelius, and the Ethiopian eunuch each took his own special path to Christ. So too evangelist Billy Graham, Joni Eareckson, William Murray (outspoken atheist Madalyn Murray O'Hair's son), Charles Colson. This choice of a few of the more prominent examples does not invalidate the less prominent. Each Christian has his or her own story, although some testimonies are more dramatic than others. What is to be stressed is the vast diversity of individuals and their unique pathways to Christ. Sensitivity to the person before us when we share our faith in Christ is vital. This is even more so for international students who have a markedly different cultural heritage, experiences, values from that of a North American Christian.

Two, a distinct sense of a spiritual journey is evident. Circumstances, people, literature and the work of the Holy Spirit play vital roles in directing a person's steps to Christ. Then comes the road to growth in Christ. Evangelism must be seen in this context. We should not glamorize the "decision for Christ" stage and forget the command to disciple new believers.

The concept of a spiritual journey suggests that conversion is often a gradual process. In a study of the decision processes of theological students, psychologist Geoffrey Scobie found gradual conversion to be the most common phenomenon. He says, "The process or growth of belief extends over a period of time, days, months, or even years. During the period the person moves from a position where he is rejecting Christianity as a whole, or some specific part of it, to a point where this rejection has changed to acceptance. There may be a climax to the process similar to the sudden conversion experience, but any such climax is secondary to the process itself. The process is of prime importance and represents a means whereby the most complicated series of objections to Christian faith can be resolved and commitment accepted."[1]

C. S. Lewis is an example of a person who went through

a gradual conversion experience. In his preface to *George MacDonald: An Anthology*, Lewis outlines the role MacDonald played in his conversion. Lewis had often seen a copy of MacDonald's *Phantastes* at a particular bookstall. He had rejected it on a dozen previous occasions before he, almost unwillingly, bought it. Says Lewis, "A few hours later I knew that I had crossed a great frontier."[2]

This great frontier didn't divide belief and unbelief in Christ. "Nothing," Lewis states, "was at that time further from my thoughts than Christianity."[3] All he was aware of was that *Phantastes* introduced him to a strange new world. This world was "homely and humble; that if this was a dream, it was a dream in which one at least felt strangely vigilant; that the whole book had about it a sort of cool, morning innocence, and also, quite unmistakably, a certain quality of Death, *good* Death."[4] What *Phantastes* did for Lewis was "to convert, even to baptise (that was where the Death came in) my imagination."[5] Lewis recounts other frontiers that lay before him: "It did nothing to my intellect nor (at that time) to my conscience. Their turn came later and with the help of many other books and men."[6]

When Lewis crossed the final frontier and entered the kingdom of God, he says, "I found that I was still with MacDonald and that he had accompanied me all the way and that I was now at last ready to hear from him much that he could not have told me at that first meeting. But in a sense, what he was now telling me was the very same that he had told me from the beginning."[7]

An awareness that conversion is often a gradual process suggests that a negative response from a non-Christian does not mean that we have failed. We could have attempted to elicit a commitment to Christ when the other person still has many unanswered objections to Christianity. A negative answer should not do irreparable damage to our relationship with the non-Christian nor should we feel disillusioned with our evangelistic abilities.

Studying the American's Language and Religion

Most international students tend to believe that just about all Americans are Christians. After all, churches dot the American landscape, especially within the vicinity of a campus. And there are few prominent signs of other varieties of religious life. Christianity is also regarded as the White man's religion by some countries, as missionaries used to be associated with Europe and the United States. Their belief may render them open to Bible study.

Yi-Qiang Xiong came to the United States for Ph.D. studies in grain science. He is a non-Christian but attends a Bible study organized by his American friends together with other students from China. Christianity is not totally new to Xiong. When "Silent Night" was sung at a church service, he recognized the tune but not the words. He last heard the carol thirty-three years ago when he was in elementary school in China. His wife (she and their two children had remained in China) wrote that the tune was also played over television in China. Xiong says he attends the Bible study unless he is too busy. His aim is "to learn something of the customs and religion of Americans."[8]

When asked if he is a Christian, Xiong laughs. It isn't a derisive laugh. It is gentle and apologetic. "No," he replies. "Not yet."

Xiong's "not yet" could mean that he is on the verge of making a decision for Christ. But the tone of his voice seems to convey the nonverbal message that he is being polite. He has some way to go in his spiritual pilgrimage. To corner him with the aim of drawing a commitment to Christ from him would only be to harvest corn when it puts forth flowers. Fortunately a more fruitful line of action is taken. Xiong's wish to learn something of the customs and religion of Americans is honored. It provides an excellent opportunity for the Christian to study the Word of God with him.

Xiong's sentiment is natural. Tourists who visit Singapore are eager to know the customs, culture and religions of Singaporeans. International students could likewise be just as curious about these things as tourists.

As for the Bible study content, it is best to design the initial material so that it is as meaningful as possible to the students. For example, Leviticus 19:33-34 is a suitable starting point: "When a stranger sojourns with you in your land, you shall not do him wrong. The stranger who sojourns with you shall be to you as the native among you, and you shall love him as yourself." The students could be asked what the verses mean. Let them perceive for themselves the verses' relevance to their circumstances. You may then discuss your relationship with them in the context of these verses. They could be encouraged to share their experiences. Do people in their home countries treat strangers in the way the Bible suggests? What sort of treatment have they received in the United States? How would they prefer to be treated?

Next, international students could be assisted to see that God's love for the stranger is not an isolated concern. A wrap-up verse to discuss is Ephesians 2:12. It refers to the "strangers to the covenants of promise." The testimonies of Christians in the Bible study group may be given at this point. How did each Christian lose his or her stranger status?

Some studies on Christ may be introduced. Here are three topics. First, the Good Samaritan story (Lk 10:25-37). It demonstrates Jesus' brilliant perception of the real issues in life, his ability to tell an incisive story, and his capacity for giving clear advice. A discussion on "Who is my neighbor?" is a suitable follow-up. Jesus' parable, told to the Jews, shows that it is possible to transcend cultural, racial and geographic barriers. Crosscultural friendship can be stressed.

Second, Jesus' discourse with the woman of Samaria (Jn 4:1-42). Jesus' sensitivity and compassion touched the woman. This incident points out how he bridges moral and cultural chasms that were much deeper than the well at Sychar. The nature of sin may be discussed.

Third, Jesus' discourse with Nicodemus (Jn 3:1-21). This contains one of the most quoted Bible verses (Jn 3:16) and the popular expression *born again.* The discussion could focus on how a person becomes a Christian.

The emphasis in this series of studies is to light the path to Christ for non-Christian international students. They may also learn to distinguish between American culture and Christianity. Our responsibilities are to give instruction on how to accept Christ as Savior, to pray for students and to provide practical help in daily living. Sensitivity to their responses will help us know if they should be asked to make a commitment to Christ. But students should not be forced to make a decision for Christ. They may enter struggling and kicking into the kingdom of God. But no Christian should attempt to drag them to God.

Besides the opportunity to learn the customs and religion of Americans, Xiong is appreciative of language help. He says, "The church group is very friendly and helps us in our language problems."

Xiong's difficulty in coping with English is acute as he comes from a non-English-speaking country. The small group Bible study session could sometimes double as a language class. Or else separate language classes could be held to help international students.

I was at the University of Chicago when I noticed an advertisement posted on a bulletin board. On it was a sketch of a guy holding a placard with the words, "TUTOR FOR JAPANESE—by a native speaker." The advertiser said, "I come from Japan. I want to teach you Japanese language for the purpose of improving my English skill. (I'm a native speaker.) Call me any time." The bottom portion of his advertisement was cut into strips. His phone number was on each strip. That certainly is an open invitation for help.

Hospitality in the United States

Professor David Sanford was in my apartment in Wheaton when Pam and I mentioned that we were planning to drive from Chicago to Los Angeles in the summer with two of our

Southeast Asian friends. He immediately invited us to stay at his Phoenix home. That invitation led to several days of hot fellowship.

"Be it ever so humble, there is no place like home" is a sentiment that assumes poignant significance for international students who suddenly find themselves relocated thousands of miles away from home. The impact is increased if they come from an extended family situation. Homesickness tends to be a common ailment. Its intensity is sharpest in their initial months in the United States. Part of the cure lies within the walls of Christian homes.

Thousands of international students have appreciated American hospitality. This is evident in two programs that cater to international students over the Christmas holidays. First, Friendship International House is a foreign student program of the Southern Baptist Convention. Nell Magee, a consultant of the convention's International Student Ministries in Nashville, says that students are assigned to a host family or a church dorm in a number of cities in the United States and Canada for twelve days over Christmas. Lodging, food and program are free. But the students have to pay a small application fee and the round trip to the city they are assigned to. No distinction is made between Christian and non-Christian students when applications are processed. Friendship is emphasized in this program.[9]

Magee says applicants have always exceeded the hosts available since FIH started in 1972. In Christmas 1981 over five hundred students participated while more than two hundred and fifty were turned down because of inadequate facilities.

A student who took part in the program wrote, "After I spent two weeks with my host family, the Gentrys, it seems to me that I have known them for a long time. If your program's purpose is to create human relationship, I would say you have met your goal perfectly. They treated us like their own children and we also feel that they are our second parents. They are beautiful people."[10]

Second, Christmas International House, a program that began in 1965, has its coordinating office within the General Assembly Mission Board of the Presbyterian Church in Atlanta, Georgia. Seven other denominations have cooperated in planning and participating in its Christmas program. About twelve hundred international students took part in this event over Christmas 1981 while nearly nine hundred were not able to get in. Again, the students were not accepted because of inadequate volunteers to host them.

These Christmas programs are community-service, not evangelism, oriented. They emphasize dialog and an exchange of ideas. Christmas of course provides an obvious occasion to talk of Christ. Commercialization celebrates the god of the shopping mall rather than God in the highest. But the Christians in their home can easily restore Christ to Christmas. It may be enlightening to ask what Christmas means to the guest. The atmosphere of a home renders it an ideal environment to talk of that which is close to our hearts.

A God-centered Christian home also provides a good witness to the non-Christian. Joseph Bayly says, "Since many international students are interested in being in an American home, I personally feel that Christian homes are some of the healthier types of homes here in the United States for them to be invited to."[11]

Besides these Christmas programs, evangelism parties could also be held in the home. The warmth of a home, the greater potential for interpersonal interaction to take place and the readiness of international students to go to an American home make it a viable option. An invitation to non-Christian students should state if a professor or other person will give a talk on Christianity. The non-Christians should be given the option to refuse such an invitation rather than find themselves the object of a talk.

Betsy Guffey, wife of the president of International Students Incorporated, gives us some tips on the practice of hospitality. Qualifications for bringing the world to your home include "a

Christ-centered home; playful children; time to share your interests, hopes and faith; and some extra chicken or pie."[12] Her next advice is to just be yourself.

As for sharing Christian beliefs she suggests, "Pray for God's love to shine through you and don't be surprised at anything that happens. Rely on the children as wonderful icebreakers. Who could resist a little wiggler climbing up on his knee or an ambitious eight-year-old explaining the wonders of model airplanes? Remember that *love* is the key. Your visitors can outwit your logic, but they have no answer for your love."[13]

Dietary restrictions should be observed. Muslims and Jews do not eat pork. Hindus do not eat beef. When my wife and I invite American friends to our apartment, we usually ask if they enjoy Chinese cuisine or prefer something American. Thus far we haven't come across an American who has not opted for Chinese food. Likewise, an American inviting an international student for a meal could freely inquire about his or her diet.

When I came to the United States, I looked upon myself as a guest. There was only one problem. For the first two years of my stay in Wheaton the vast majority of American Christians did not look upon themselves as hosts. On the occasions when some of them did feel that they should perhaps play the part of hosts, their feelings were not translated into action. Jeff was my immediate apartment neighbor. For more than six months he would say, "My wife and I want to invite you and your wife over to our apartment." He said it so often whenever we met that he had to vary his invitation a little: "I want you to know that I haven't forgotten about my invitation." Pam and I finally decided to take the initiative. We invited them as well as two other American couples over to our apartment for dinner. When Jeff left Wheaton, I still had not seen the inside of his apartment. He did not peg his intention to a specific date.

Hospitality occasionally presents the hosts with rare rewards. Scripture tells of instances of those who entertained angels unawares. Abraham and Lot are two examples. In the case of Cleopas and his companion, they entertained a resurrected

Christ without realizing it. Not all strangers are angels or the Messiah. They may not even be angelic or Christlike. What should be remembered is that our mission in this world is, after all, to minister to those who are a little lower than the angels. This includes international students.

Marks of a True Dialog

Dialog is a useful way of presenting our Christian beliefs and experiences with international students. John Stott presents four arguments in favor of dialog.[14] First, true dialog is a mark of authenticity. We do not merely proclaim the gospel to non-Christians from a distance. We draw near to them. Our masks come down. We begin to be seen and known for what we are. Mutual understanding is fostered as the conversation develops. We come to respect their convictions, their culture, to feel with their pain and struggles. We still want to communicate the good news to them, for we care deeply about it. Yet at the same time we also care about the non-Christians with whom we want to share the gospel.

Second, true dialog is a mark of humility. As we listen to others, our respect for them as human beings made in God's image grows. The gap brought about by differences in color of skin, accent and mannerisms diminishes. We realize that we cannot sweep away all their cherished convictions with a brash, unfeeling dismissal. We have to recognize that their misconceptions of Christianity may be our fault. Our attitude about them changes. Any lingering sense of superiority of which we were previously unconscious is removed. We no longer desire to score points to win a debate. Humility in evangelism is a beautiful grace.

Third, true dialog is a mark of integrity. This is the usual outcome of our conversation. We listen to our friends' real beliefs and problems. We also divest our minds of the false images we may have harbored. At the same time we ourselves are determined to be real.

Fourth, true dialog is a mark of sensitivity. Evangelism falls into disrepute when we attempt to evangelize by fixed formulae. The very essence of dialog, however, is an attempt at mutual listening. This makes it possible to react sensitively both to the actual needs of our friends and to the guidance of the Holy Spirit.

Scripture shows the validity of the use of dialog. In his second missionary journey Paul spent three weeks in the synagogue at Thessalonica. There "he argued with them from the scriptures, explaining and proving that it was necessary for the Christ to suffer and to rise from the dead, and saying, 'This Jesus, whom I proclaim to you, is the Christ.' " Luke then tells us the outcome: "And some of them were persuaded" (Acts 17:1-4). Paul's dialog suggests that he listens to the objections to the claims of Christ raised by his hearers. He then argues, explains, proves, proclaims and persuades. Paul's dialog with his audience has two main characteristics. The subject of his dialog is Jesus Christ. The object is belief in Christ.

The concept of dialog has, however, taken a different meaning in the past few decades. Dialog is sometimes advocated by those who hold the opinion that the Christian faith and non-Christian faiths are alternative and equally valid roads to God. They are very tolerant and accommodating toward the teachings of other religions, and they compromise Christianity in their attempt to unite or reconcile all religions. This is syncretism. Evangelicals are compelled to oppose this idea of ecumenical dialog. True Christian dialog with a non-Christian is not an indulgence in syncretism. We remain consistent to our belief in the uniqueness of what Christ has done for us and humanity.

An Introduction to Church Fellowship
Thus far, attention has been centered mainly on imparting the gospel at a personal level. Another approach is to expose our friends to the public proclamation of the gospel. This can be done in two contexts. First, the preaching of the gospel or the ministry of the Word within the church. Second, the proclama-

tion of the Christian faith on the secular campus by professors.

Most people are prepared to do almost anything once. For non-Christians this includes going to a church service. Having said this, it is nevertheless helpful not to invite our friends merely to a "church service." It is usually better to invite them to hear a specific talk given by a particular person in a church. We then tell our friends as much as possible of the subject and the speaker. If they do not wish to accept the invitation, they merely say no to an invitation rather than to attending a church service. They could then be extended further invitations at a time more convenient to them. But if they do have strong objections to going to church, their feelings should be respected.

We also need to find out if our friends have ever attended any church service before. And if they have, whether they are familiar with the order of service in the church we are inviting them to. If they are not, we need to explain what they could expect. For instance, when do we stand, sit, kneel, bow our heads and close our eyes, recite, sing? What is the significance of what we do in church? We must remember that what is familiar to us may be puzzling and disconcerting to our friends. Since we do not wish to invite them to church in order to embarrass them, we have to be sensitive to their need for fairly detailed information on what to expect in a service. It puts them at ease. They do not have to launch completely into the unknown.

If there is a coffee or fellowship hour after the service, we should also remain with our friends rather than wander off to visit with other Christians. Our presence with our guests is an indication of our courtesy toward them. They seldom appreciate being left alone to fend for themselves. This suggestion is applicable even if we have invited two or more friends. It is also a good practice to introduce them to our other Christian friends.

Attempt to create an atmosphere of warmth through such actions. What we do is a significant part of our witness to our friends. They need to see the quality of life within the church as well as hear our message. We would want to help them to come, see and taste of Christian fellowship. And to go away with the idea that our fellowship is good.

A follow-up step we could take is to discuss this common experience. We might talk about the content of the preacher's message and their impressions of the church and its people. The discussion will help us to gain some insights into our friends' spiritual state: Do they understand the fundamentals of the gospel? Do they perceive any relevance in the message? Is there any attempt at personal application? We could also try to correct any misconceptions they may have. Or we may perceive that they are ready to commit their lives to Christ. We should then encourage them to make this life-transforming decision.

Professors Challenge Secularism

The public proclamation of the Christian world view and belief on the secular campus by professors is a less common approach but has the potential for making an impact on international students. One of the most striking examples took place on the University of Wisconsin-Madison campus. *Christianity Challenges the University* tells how five senior professors at the university confronted the campus community with the truth of Christianity.[15]

The professors believe that all cultures have their gods, and the god of secular culture is humanity. In the secular culture of today's university every value becomes subordinated to that god. The only knowledge that matters is knowledge that directly benefits or glorifies humanity. This posed a dilemma for them. To speak out and oppose such values was to go against the academic grain. To remain silent was to confirm for the students the assumption that the beliefs of secularism are unchallenged and unchallengeable.

A response to this dilemma then took shape. Dr. Wilkes writes, "One group of professors on the Madison, Wisconsin, campus who had been meeting regularly for prayer felt them-

selves called to make some sort of public statement. The possi-
bility was approached somewhat nervously. After all, to get
a name for religious enthusiasm is not likely to enhance one's
academic career. But the imperatives of our situation were
clear, and in the end we could do no other."[16]

They selected a title for the series, assigned the subjects,
booked the Great Hall of the Memorial Union, and sought the
help of Christian students in distributing posters. Each week for
five successive Monday lunchtimes they were overwhelmed
with student response. They had, in faith, asked the Union for
two hundred chairs. The seating was totally inadequate. The
chairs had to be more than doubled. The floor, windowsills and
stairs held the overflow.

Each professor spoke on a different topic. Dr. Wilkes posed
the Christian world view as a radical alternative to secular
humanism. Dr. Wayne Becker, professor of botany, contrasted
the secular and Christian views of human nature. Dr. David
Richardson, professor of economics, confronted current
economic dogmas. Dr. Keith Schoville, professor of Hebrew
and Semitic studies, summarized the evidence for the reliability
of scriptural documents. Dr. A. A. MacKinney, professor of
medicine, outlined the Christian notion of a whole person and
critiqued the contemporary models of modern medicine.

"When it was all over," concludes Dr. Wilkes, "we came to the
conviction that what we had done could be done at any
university. When a group of professors, including distinguished
scholars, takes the opportunity to speak out in the university,
others will listen. We acknowledge that the step was a small one,
but it is our hope that by many such small steps the journey to
the kingdom may be made."[17]

Let me add two observations. First, most international
students come from countries where professors are highly
respected, authoritative figures. This means that they may be
more willing to accept an invitation to hear a professor give a
talk, even on a religious topic, than an invitation to hear a
pastor preach in a church. Where Christian professors do not

take the initiative, they could be recruited to witness in this
fashion.

Second, *Christianity Challenges the University* or similar books
may make a suitable gift for any of our friends who are
interested in topics addressed by Christian professors. The
content of such books could become the launching point for
a discussion on Christian beliefs. The event itself, of course,
makes a good topic for discussion. Why did these professors
bother to do what they did? Their willingness to act on what
they believe authenticates their faith.

Such formal proclamations of the gospel are likely to help
those who are already prepared to receive the good news of
salvation. For those who are still some distance from belief,
such exposure could be used to clarify their thoughts and
feelings on basic Christian beliefs.[18] Our Christian mission is
to be faithful in helping our friends to understand the gospel
of Jesus Christ.

CHAPTER 6

PROSELYTIZE IS A DIRTY WORD

THE WORD *PROSELYTIZE* IS A BLARING SIREN TO A ZEALOUS ANTI-Christian. Strident, uncompromising, unrelenting, it screams for attention. We can't disregard this fact. We need to overcome a natural tendency to dismiss the words and deeds of those who oppose us, to rationalize our own shortcomings and look upon them in the best possible light.

Guidelines for Community Groups
The National Association for Foreign Student Affairs (NAFSA), a professional organization exclusively devoted to international educational interchange, was formed in 1948. It was then called the National Association of Foreign Student Advisers. NAFSA comprises five professional sections: admissions officers, teachers of English as a second language, advisers to international students and scholars, advisers to United States students on study abroad, and the representatives of community organizations that provide services and programs for international students in the United States.

NAFSA's importance lies partly in its role as an association that attempts to define responsibilities and maintain standards in international student interchange. Its guidelines on religious and political groups are noteworthy:

> Community workers related to religious and political groups must recognize that the religious and political beliefs of any foreign people in the United States are important parts of their cultural heritage and merit the respect of Americans and the effort by Americans to learn about and understand them. Religious and political groups can provide a service by providing opportunities for foreign students and scholars to observe and join in mutual inquiry into beliefs and practices. However, there must never be any attempt to proselyte, and any invitation to a foreign student or scholar to an event sponsored by a religious or political group should clearly indicate the nature of the event and its sponsorship.[1]

These are guidelines which the Association of Christian Ministries to Internationals (ACMI) encourages its members to observe. ACMI interprets the word "proselyte" to mean "to manipulate and pressure an individual in an attempt to cause him to change."[2] This interpretation diffuses the explosive quality of the guidelines. It also increases their acceptability.

NAFSA places laudable emphasis on Americans' respecting, learning, and understanding the cultural heritage of international students. An attempt to learn another culture is beneficial to American Christians. They are likely to gain insights into their own culture, question values which they may not even know they possess because they grew up with them, and enlarge their perceptions of the world.

NAFSA is also wise to suggest that international students be given the opportunity to observe and join in mutual inquiry into beliefs and practices. No one likes being buttonholed. Mutual inquiry implies a nonpatronizing, nonarrogant approach.

Most international students are curious about religious matters and are usually willing to attend meetings where the gospel will be preached—if accompanied by their friend. To invite an international student to a social and then spring a surprise gospel presentation on him or her is not only unnecessary but may also harm the relationship. The NAFSA guideline is a sensible one.

Some Concerns of Secular Authorities

An article in the February 1983 issue of *NAFSA Newsletter* presents a fairly comprehensive secular concern and perspective toward activities of Christians on the campus.[3] It begins, "Fundamentalist Christian groups are actively approaching international students studying at Iowa State University. This may be part of a nationwide campaign on many college and university campuses. While these efforts may be only friendly welcomes to international visitors, they may also be preludes to heavy proselytizing."

"Friendly welcomes" are encouraged. "Heavy proselytizing" is discouraged.

Two plausible reasons are given for the wish to safeguard international students from proselytizing. First, "a concern that some students undergoing adjustment to university life in the United States may experience serious psychological harm if subjected to a hard sell from Christian groups." Second, "an international student at Iowa State University was giving large sums of money meant for his tuition to one of the groups."

"Some students" sounds vague. And one international student does not seem an awfully large number. Statistics, however, do not play a key role in the argument, especially since they appeared to be scanty.

Two observations may be made. First, a few complaints from students who have had distasteful encounters with supersalesmen of Christianity could alarm university administrators entrusted with their welfare. Exaggeration is a common human failing. A few complaints can sometimes generate enough hot air to launch a thousand balloons. (Perhaps *I* exaggerate.) Second, the concerns are nevertheless real and should be viewed as such. The grievance is far more important than the number of complainants.

Sensitivity is helpful when confronted with administrators in a secular organization who wish to safeguard an international student's cultural heritage. Our commission to evangelize does not authorize us to do so in an obnoxious, overbearing, domineering fashion. We are to be lights, not to blind non-Christians but to illuminate the pathway to Christ.

The writers of the article mention two undesirable options that university administrators could make. They could cooperate indiscriminately with religious groups. Or they could refuse to work with any religious organizations and try to protect international students from such influence.

Instead, the writers advocate reasoned discriminate judgments on the motivations, intentions and goals of the religious groups desiring to work with international students. They raise three questions.

First, "Does the motivation for involvement with international students stem from a *missionary* or *service* orientation?" A missionary orientation is defined as one that "seeks to work through college and university programs as a means to proselytize." A service orientation "attempts to assist a college or university in its work with international students without expectation of gaining new converts."

They provide this example: "There is a difference between a conservative Christian fellowship group that has targeted international students as likely objects for evangelism, and a nearby campus church whose members volunteer for language assistance programs as an expression of hospitality."

The writers assume that the only legitimate involvement with internationals stems from a service orientation. Any missionary orientation is automatically suspect. As Christians we must disagree. We believe that God has called us not only to serve international students but also to share the gospel with them. Of course we should not treat them as *objects* of evangelism. They are *people* with needs—one of which is their need for Jesus Christ. We serve them by sharing the good news about

Christ without neglecting their other needs.

Second, "Is the intent a *paternalistic presentation of a particular religious perspective,* or a *mutually educative process?*" A paternalistic presentation of religion "attempts to prove its superiority in comparison with other religious traditions." On the other hand, in a mutually educative process "both parties respect the integrity of each other's religion, and both expect to learn something about different faith positions."

They note the difference between a campus religious group that "entices international students to a dinner and then offers a heavy sales pitch, and a group that sets up a dialogue program where various religious perspectives are discussed. The former ignores the religion of international students, while the latter desires a mutual exchange of information."

Much of this criticism is valid. Trickery is to be abhorred. Christianity is not a product to be sold. As for Christianity's superiority, it is the students who should be given the prerogative to decide. But they need to be conversant with the teachings of Christ before they can make any judgments. This is where the Christian serves international students by providing them with the knowledge they need to make an informed choice.

Third, "Is the goal to have international students *adopt a new religious perspective* or *affirm the one they possess?*" In the former, "there is an implicit assumption that a particular religious perspective possesses the 'truth,' and those outside do not. It is a denial of religious pluralism." The latter "implies that 'truth' is relative. The religious perspectives of international students are therefore respected. Religious pluralism is endorsed. There is a major difference between tolerating 'foreign religions' as misguided perspectives that are 'correctable,' and affirming other religions as legitimate and valuable expressions."

Again, it is international students who must decide for themselves after they have grasped the essential facts.

The writers assume that all international students have a personal religious heritage. I have found that this is not so.

They also assume that international students are quite helpless creatures. They certainly are in dire need of help in their initial adjustment period. But once they come to know the system, they can beat their American counterparts in the game. They are not part of the intellectual elite of their country without reasonable grounds.

Christian activities tend to be high profile. They are thus more easily attacked. International students, however, face less overt influences. Drugs, materialism and sexual permissiveness are insidious moral forces that administrators should display equal concern for. A student from China, for instance, asked a Christian professor for Christian roommates for his friends from China. Christians, he said, do not steal or cheat—they are kind.

The writers conclude on the note that they do not advocate that religious expression or activity on campus be severely limited. They readily admit, "There are constitutional guarantees that prohibit such an endeavor."

College and university administrators need community assistance if they are to be effective in their attempt to enrich the life of international students on their campus. Just handling the legal and administrative problems of the students could take up all their time.

On the other hand, it is preferable that church leaders who wish to commit their members to help international students should maintain a working relationship with the administrators in the Foreign Student Office. Dialog begins at this level.

Troublemakers or Messengers of Grace?

How do we answer the charges of those who accuse us of seeking converts and of denying religious pluralism because of our belief in the uniqueness of Christianity? Expressing his insights into the meaningless cycle of life, the writer of Ecclesiastes states, "What has been is what will be, and what has been done is what will be done; and there is nothing new under the sun" (1:9). Certainly there is nothing new in charges

being leveled against Christians who preach the gospel of Jesus
Christ. One example in Paul's second missionary journey
stands out. It took place in Thessalonica, the capital city of
Macedonia.

Paul's strategy was to begin his ministry in a synagogue. He
consequently spent three sabbaths evangelizing among those
who attended the synagogue. His arguments, explanations and
proofs led many to believe in Christ. Paul's effective preaching,
however, aroused the jealousy of the Jews. Enlisting the help of
some rabble-rousers, the Jews created an uproar. The accusa-
tion that the Jews leveled at all who were involved with Paul was
that they "caused trouble everywhere" (Acts 17:6 TEV).

The Jews were envious of Paul because "a great many of the
devout Greeks and not a few of the leading women" (Acts 17:4)
were being drawn away from the synagogue. These Gentiles
were potential converts to Judaism. In their desperate attempt
to stem the movement of Gentiles away from Judaism, the Jews
resorted to foul means to achieve their goal.

In the eyes of the Jews, Paul was a rival, a troublemaker. In
the eyes of the converts, Paul was a missionary, a messenger of
God. False accusations should not deter us from ministering to
international students. We have been given spiritual power to
preach the gospel of Christ.

Commenting on potential tension between Christians and
foreign student advisers, Joseph Bayly says, "That's where you
have to know whether God has called you into this ministry. If
he has then, as nicely as possible, you have to say, 'I'm sorry,
I have a personal responsibility that I feel toward international
students. I'm not trying to take away from what you are doing
with international students but you are not the only person on
campus who has a concern for them.' "[4]

We also need to ensure that we are not wrongly or mistakenly
motivated. John Stott puts it thus: "We must refuse to try to
bludgeon people into the kingdom of God. The very attempt is
an insult to the dignity of human beings and a sinful usurpation
of the prerogatives of the Holy Spirit. It is also unproductive.

For one inevitable result of evangelism by unlawful means (what Paul called 'disgraceful, underhanded ways' 2 Corinthians 4:2) is the leakage from the church of those whose conversion has thus been 'engineered.' "[5]

Faithfulness—not worldly success—is praised by Christ in his parable of the talents (Mt 25:21). Ned Hale cautions against the success-oriented American mindset. Before coming on IVCF staff Hale had already been involved in crosscultural work in his undergraduate days at Yale University and then at Fuller Theological Seminary. Afterward, "Quite frankly, I had a lot to learn about myself and about the ministry, and I learned them those first few years while I was on staff." He had to learn "how American I am." He elaborates,

By that I mean how vehemently I wanted to succeed in the ministry. That militated against any kind of failure, particularly in terms of conversions of international students. I longed to see many become Christians. I naively believed, even felt, that God was speaking to me, that I would see fifty become Christians in the first year of ministry. But God graciously allowed me to see three people become Christians.

As I came to learn later, it is a miracle of God—every time a student becomes a Christian. It isn't something one can humanly generate. I knew that theologically, but existentially it didn't grip me until, in the ministry, I suddenly came face to face with the fact that I wasn't going to convert these students to Jesus Christ. God is the one who gets the credit for it.

And one of the things we learn in international student ministry is to trust God to work even when it isn't apparent that much is happening. That is a difficult kind of lesson for an American to learn. And yet that is vital for any lasting commitment to a ministry that calls upon you to have a great deal of patience, faithfulness, and trust in the Lord, that he is using you when the results do not appear to be very significant.[6]

CHAPTER 7

PREPARING FOR RE-ENTRY

ONE OF MY JAPANESE FRIENDS WHO STUDIED IN THE UNITED STATES for sixteen months was acutely aware of the changes that had taken place in her perceptions and values. "Pray for me" was her request when she completed her graduate studies and prepared to return home. She knew that she was about to re-enter a very conservative society where women performed a very low-profile social function. She had come to value the American lifestyle for women. Niceties such as men opening the door of the car for her, being treated as an equal companion while on dates and the freedom of doing what struck her fancy would be excess baggage to be left behind when she boarded the plane for Japan. She did not relish the thought of undergoing the anticipated shock of re-entry.

A broad range of adjustment patterns to life in the United States may be noted among international students. On one end of the continuum are those who unreservedly immerse themselves in American society. They seek out the company of

Americans and may dissociate themselves from other international students, including those of their own nationality, unless they too are committed to talking and behaving like Americans. This category of students is more noticeable among the impressionable teen-age undergraduates than the more staid, older graduate students. Such wholehearted acceptance of the American way of life will bring about substantial changes in their personality. This invariably results in sizeable readjustment difficulties when they return home.

At the other end of the continuum are international students who safeguard themselves against change. They deliberately shun American company, continue to talk and behave the way they did in their home country, and generally attempt to transplant their former lifestyle into American soil. This is usually more feasible for a married couple. They provide mutual support for one another and can live fairly comfortably in their own way. They face minimal readjustment pains when they return home.

Most international students, however, do not insulate themselves against the onslaught of change. When this happens, readjustment to their former or primary culture becomes necessary when they return. Just as culture shock is a term used for the dynamics of entry into a new culture, re-entry shock denotes the readjustment process. Both the initial and later adjustments are just as disconcerting and frustrating for students who are not prepared for them.

Alienation or Reversion
"Change and decay in all around I see" is the melancholic lament of hymn writer Henry Lyte. Although the context is different, international students who return home after an absence of several years may be overwhelmed by a similar sentiment. An era has seemingly slipped by. Time had not stood still in their own countries while they were in the United States. Reverse culture shock is heightened if political upheavals or unexpected changes in society have taken place during

their sojourn in the United States. Re-entry therefore can be as critical and traumatic as the earlier adjustment to the American way of life.

Pleasant emotions usually predominate in the initial phase of returnees' arrival home. There really is no place like home when looked at from a long way off. Reunion with family and friends is a happy occasion. A sense of academic or professional achievement adds to the glow.

Warm, fuzzy, fantasy feelings, however, are balloons that are soon burst by the sharp needles of reality. Students rapidly awaken to a changed home environment. Job hunting may degenerate into a chore that may puncture optimistic expectations. Frustration often follows an inability to secure a career in a chosen field of specialization.

Other tensions confront returnees. Their peers are often unable to relate to their overseas experiences and may express superficial comments on their adventures abroad. They are left with no one with whom they can speak intelligibly of their past years in the United States. Feelings of superiority because of their having lived and traveled abroad, coupled with feelings of jealousy on the part of their peers who lack opportunities for studying overseas, sour relationships.

Changes have taken place in the students themselves. They may realize that their years away from home have perceptibly and radically or subtly left their marks on them. One possible change: they may talk with an American accent. If their home countries have an English accent of their own, the American twang will be frowned on as a put-on and will grate on the ears and nerves of friends. While they usually lose the accent rapidly, unless they deliberately cultivate it, other changes are often less easy to shake off. Their behavior, attitudes and values may have undergone a metamorphosis.

When I was a journalist in Singapore I met a non-Christian who had studied in the United States. During our brief meeting he unhesitatingly poured vitriol on the newspaper in which I was working. He denounced it as pro-government, and said there was a lack of freedom of the press and freedom of expression in Singapore. The paper was most uninteresting, he claimed, and could be read in a mere ten minutes. "When I was in the United States," he said, "I sometimes spent the whole Sunday just reading the papers." In his harangue all things Singaporean were dull and ugly. All things American were bright and beautiful.

This type of re-entry is referred to as alienation.[1] Alienated returnees react negatively to their home culture. On the one hand, they carp at its values, beliefs and norms. On the other hand, they glorify the American culture, beliefs and values that they have imbued. They tend to reject alternatives for resolving personal, social, economic and political concerns.

Alienation stands at one end of the readjustment process. At the other extreme is reversion. Here the returnees revert to values, beliefs and norms they held before their crosscultural experience. They reject any changes which may have occurred while they were in the United States. Except for their academic or professional degree, they seem not to have left the shores of their own country.

Both alienation and reversion are ways of coping with re-entry that, at best, reduces the beneficial effects of a crosscultural experience. They reflect an absence of a sustained effort to grapple creatively with and attempt to resolve the tensions of having lived in another culture.

Each of these re-entry styles may not be manifested exclusively. Returnees may exhibit, at various times, either alienation or reversion. But there is a third and preferred style.

Returning to Orbit without Burnout

Re-entry into the orbit of their former circuit can fortunately be achieved without a fiery burnout. They can undergo a process of integration. They view their return home as another transitional period. Their academic or professional studies overseas are over, but they know that their education continues. Their return home provides further opportunities for learning and change. They attempt to integrate their learning in a foreign culture with life in their primary culture. Neither is viewed as superior to the other.

Here we have another possible ministry to international students. We can help make them aware of the pleasures and pains of re-entry even before they leave American airspace. Those who are prepared will usually be better able to maneuver themselves safely as they plunge back into their own country's airspace. A knowledge of potential difficulties ahead alerts their perceptions and sensitivities. When these surface they are not taken unawares. And they may have solutions to some of them. This of course is the desirable approach.

When I left Singapore for the United States I expected to be away for five years without much likelihood of seeing my homeland in between. I know the rapid, relentless pace of change in my country. I knew that I would return home to, in a sense, a new country, a new church and a new family. Events thus far have not disappointed me. Singapore became the second busiest port in the world, an airport reputed to be one of the most efficient in the world was opened, Singapore's president died and a new president was installed, and a number of rising political stars fell. My church saw the resignation of nine deacons, new members were added, one of my church elders died and a building program within the church compound was underway. On the home front, both my parents were baptized, two of my sisters-in-law had a baby each and my father had a mild stroke. All these events and much more have already taken place within my first three years away from home.

Realizing that a Rip Van Winkle gap in our lives may occur, my wife and I resolved to keep the postal authorities busy. Constant correspondence with family and friends means that although we are away in body we can be present in spirit. The venerable Rip was away both in body and spirit for twenty years. And a revolution came and went. Knowing that revolutions revolve at a much faster rate nowadays, we are even more eager to be kept informed of political, socioeconomic, religious and educational changes in Singapore and the neighboring countries. This is especially so as Southeast Asian countries are accorded honorable but fleeting mention by the American mass media once in a long interval.

Another step that we have taken is to request free publications that our government puts out. Although they are considered government propaganda, any news is better than no news. We also receive newsletters from a number of churches and organizations. They again help us keep abreast of people and events. Through such means we hope to have a skeletal idea of what is taking place in our years away from Singapore. These are suggestions you could easily pass on to your international friends, or you could even write for the materials for them.

Attitudes are also important. International students who look forward to their return home and anticipate a transitional period of readjustment are likely to reintegrate with less pain into their primary society and culture. On the other hand, students who view their homeward journey with foreboding may unconsciously wish to perceive only negative features in their country. This selective perception may reinforce their apprehensions, pride, prejudices.

Two pertinent scriptural verses are, "Be watchful, stand firm in your faith, be courageous, be strong. Let all that you do be done in love" (1 Cor 16:13-14). Four basic but essential military commands are given to us as soldiers of Christ: be watchful, stand firm, be courageous, be strong. International students are suitably equipped for re-entry if they take to heart this exhortation. It renders them alert to changes in the environment as well as in relationships with family, friends and colleagues. This keenness of mind and spirit will help them avoid a roller-coaster adaptation to a new lifestyle.

"Let all that you do be done in love" is an important modification to the four commands. Actions motivated by love have a salutary effect on both doer and recipient.

Planning to Serve Back Home

"Some of the most positive experiences a university administrator can have is visiting his former students as they are in positions of leadership in their countries," states Dr. Marvin Mardock, director of International Studies at Azusa Pacific University, California. His negative experiences with international students "revolve around those who become materialistic or those who have lost their original vision of God's will."[2]

Preparation for re-entry by students from the same country or region can be helpful in nurturing or evoking such a vision. First, the students are often intimately acquainted with their home situation. Knowledge of the political, social, economic and religious conditions in their country would mean a more accurate anticipation and planning for the readjustment process.

Second, the more spiritually mature who have a vision for serving in their churches are in a position to enthuse the spiritually weak or young.

Third, since the students usually belong to different denominations, coming together for group planning and fellowship stresses the unity of believers. Sectarian feelings tend to run deeper in Christians who have not experienced close and warm relationships with Christians from other denominations. This sense of unity may result in greater cooperation in future inter-denominational functions.

Fourth, prayerful commitment to a life of service even before students return prepares them to order their priorities. Looking outwards to the needs of others will help them live an abundant life. Proverbs 11:24-25 says,

One man gives freely, yet grows all the richer;
    another withholds what he should give, and only suffers want.
A liberal man will be enriched,
    and one who waters will himself be watered.

A group of international students who come together with well-articulated objectives is the Singaporean Malaysian Awareness Group (SMAG). It consists of Christians from different churches involved in the Malaysian Singaporean student ministry in Toronto. One of the five goals of SMAG is "to nurture a vision for the Lord's work in each Malaysian Singaporean student as he/she returns home."

SMAG has a United Kingdom connection. It has reprinted the *Malaysian Christian Handbook,* originally produced by Malaysian students in the United Kingdom.[3] The students studying in the United Kingdom were drawn together by a common concern for the church in Malaysia and their responsibility toward it. In January 1978 they organized the first Malaysian Christian Conference sponsored by the Chinese Overseas Christian Mission. Papers presented in the 1978 and 1979 conferences were edited and compiled into a handbook. Nearly all the papers were written by Malaysian Christian students, most of whom had previous working experience. A missionary leader with extensive experience in East Asia presented one paper. The papers addressed issues that Christians face in Malaysia. One of the aims of the handbook is that of "preserving in a more permanent and compact form, a means for sharing the vision for God's work in Malaysia amongst Christian students back home and overseas."

Topics include a history of Malaysia since its independence, the Christian's response to Malaysia today, the church in Malaysia, theological education, avenues for full-time service in Malaysia, Christian perspectives to vocations, the role of women in the Malaysian church, and vision for the Malaysian church.

The concerns of the students are:

Prayerful awareness and preparation now are priorities which we ignore at our own peril—the needs of the Church in Malaysia are immensely urgent to warrant a radical change of spiritual outlook in our lives. These are threads that run all the way through the papers. The problems considered are manifold, the answers are never claimed to be final, but they testify to God's working in stirring an increasing number of Christians here to meet and think through them in the light of Scriptural principles and to act on them. If they serve to awaken us to the needs of the hour and to turn aside to pray, re-commit our lives to God and to work out fresh solutions to existing problems confronting us, then this handbook has more than justified its existence. Our greatest tragedy would be apathy and an unwillingness to get involved.[4]

Emigration and talk of emigration by the non-Malay and non-Muslim in Malaysia, especially among university graduates, are common. The Christian international students' resolve to confront, intellectually and spiritually, the problems they will face when they return to their country is commendable. Such a preparation will soften the impact of re-entry shock and also give direction to their future vocation and ministry.

What these groups of international students are doing could provide the inspiration for other Christian students to do likewise.

CHAPTER 8

THE TAUSSIGS: A MODEL COUPLE

AFTER MY FIRST VISIT TO MANHATTAN, KANSAS, I LEFT MANHATTAN Municipal Airport in a single-engine plane in which the pilot occupied twenty-five per cent of the seating capacity. But during that late-winter weekend I spent in Manhattan, I met and stayed with a couple whose home had packed in crowds ten times that which the plane was able to accommodate. Their lives have touched many more.

Happy is the man, says the psalmist, who has his quiver full of children. The Taussigs are a couple whose quiver runneth over. Besides seven children and twenty-six grandchildren, they look upon hundreds of international students as part of their extended family—their spiritual children. It is a heritage that comes from the Lord.

For the Taussigs, age was no barrier to new beginnings. Their unassuming manners, ready hospitality and venturesomeness are valuable assets. Dr. Robert Taussig, then a professor of veterinary medicine at Kansas State University,

Manhattan, and his wife Mary were also strategically located for starting a ministry among international students—on a university campus. Nevertheless, their ministry did not begin until they returned from a land where they themselves were foreigners. This tale of two compassionate hearts has a Nigerian connection.

Bringing Home a Nigerian Burden
Living in a foreign land is a vulnerable, tense, enlightening experience. What is commonplace in our own culture could be outlandishly outrageous in another. Our sensitivity to others and their reactions to us are heightened. This was so for the Taussigs when they left the sheltered environment of Manhattan in 1972 and arrived at Ahmadu Bello University in Nigeria. Dr. Taussig, on a federally funded Agency for International Development program, taught veterinary medicine at the university for four years. These were also years of learning for them. It was in Nigeria that a burden for international students fell on them.

They met many Nigerian students bitter about their experiences in the United States. Stories of loneliness, mistreatment and rejection abounded.

"I hate America," said one student. "It has nothing to offer me."

Ironically, the very country that considers itself gracious and loving in sending missionaries to less-developed countries is viewed as an ugly nation by some students who have lived in the United States. This knowledge, coupled with their firsthand perceptions of the needs in a foreign land, gave the Taussigs an added impetus for a campus ministry.

The fall of 1976 saw them back in Manhattan, and Dr. Taussig resumed his teaching position at Kansas State University.

"We returned feeling very convinced that God was leading us to do something for international students," said Dr. Taussig. "But we didn't know what to do."

They were then unaware of any ministry to international students and did not know who or where to turn for help.

Readjustment to life in Manhattan was another major preoccupation during their first year home. "We had become accustomed to the slower pace of life in Africa," he said, "and to the freedom from the telephone and television. And also to the much more social atmosphere where people relate to each other more naturally than they do in our culture."

The Burden Becomes a Vision

First in their hearts was a burden. Then their minds sought a way to lighten it. Before too long the burden was transformed into a vision to serve international students. Fully persuaded that the Lord was leading them to do something for international students, but uncertain over what to do, the Taussigs prayed. And prayed. For one year.

They obtained a list of names of international students and prayed for each person. "Each day," said Dr. Taussig, "my wife and I would name each student, on one page, before the Lord. The next day, we would turn the page and then we would pray for another group."

What germinated from the sowing of these seeds of prayer was their conviction that the students' social and cultural problems must be taken care of before spiritual needs could be addressed. This belief came out of their having lived in another culture.

"We felt that the number one thing to do was to provide a friendship-type of loving compassion where we help and serve the international student—even before we think of anything spiritual. We understood enough to realize that it was going to be very difficult to have a spiritual ministry without first having a relationship and understanding something of the culture of the student. So, from the beginning, the emphasis was on friendship."

He added, "And by friendship we mean something more than that which is casual. Genuine friendship has to have some depth and quality."

Unexpected assistance helped launch the friendship program. Three American students who lived in the basement rooms in the Taussig home became willing recruits when their hosts shared their ideas. The trio invited international students over for meals, visited them, assisted them with their shopping and with housing during breaks when dorms were closed.

More volunteers soon joined them. The scope of their activities expanded to include Bible study and evangelistic meetings held in their home. Decorated with artifacts from Africa, their home has a distinct crosscultural atmosphere.

From a Home to the Church

Objectives crystallized. This led, in the fall of 1978, to the formation of Helping International Students (HIS). The Taussigs were the first directors of this church-based community service organization.

Grace Baptist Church, an independent Baptist church that the Taussigs belong to, figured prominently in HIS activities. When the pastor first gave Dr. Taussig pulpit time in the fall 1978 semester to explain the HIS program and appeal for volunteers, eighty church members responded. Appeals were then made at the start of each semester. Four years later the number of American helpers rose to more than two hundred and seventy. More than half were Grace Baptist Church members.

Besides serving the international student community in their area, the Taussigs felt that HIS stimulated the congregation to be more missions-minded, promoted greater world awareness and provided a training and support base for crosscultural work.

They believe that the local church rather than parachurch organizations should be the base for international student work. The church's communal and family life, and manpower and financial resources, render it an ideal center for this kind of ministry.

Helping Americans to Serve

In their initial years of ministry the Taussigs designed several training programs, workshops and seminars to teach American volunteers crosscultural principles of conversation and communication.

"The American is more of a problem to us than the international," says Dr. Taussig. "The problem is with our narrow, provincial outlook; our Western culture that thinks that everything resides here. This even splinters off into the idea that Western Caucasian people are more intelligent, more sophisticated. It's a type of Western blindness."

The Taussigs outline several aims to orient their American volunteers to serve international students.[1]

First, we would like every international student to receive warm-hearted help in adjusting to the American culture, and to have the opportunity to develop a friendship with an American Christian.

Second, we would like to provide every Christian international student with the opportunity for a warm Christian fellowship, for spiritual growth and maturity in his or her personal walk with the Lord.

Third, we would like to provide every student with an opportunity to hear a faithful, intelligent presentation of the gospel of Jesus Christ given in the power of the Holy Spirit.

Fourth, we would like to provide a valid crosscultural social vehicle where Americans can gain an understanding and appreciation of other cultures and people.

Fifth, we would like the church fellowship to be able to participate in foreign missions by sharing the love of Christ with these men and women who have come here to us from other lands.

The Bonds of Friendship

Friendship on a "one-to-one" basis is the ideal the Taussigs stress in their training sessions. In this approach one American partners one international student. They observe, "This requires large numbers of Christian Americans and a working relationship with the university administration. It may not be possible on every campus and in every church group. But it's an ideal worth striving for. All the group activities, both social and spiritual, are vital, but nothing can compare with the significance of a one-to-one friendship."

The Taussigs suggest this "Bonding Process":

When American Christians have volunteered to love and serve international students, the process of matching students with their new American friends must be done carefully and prayerfully.

We consider age, geographical proximity, field of study, interests and marital status. A single male would not be paired with a single girl. Usually we would not pair an older married student with a young, single American. However, a young student may form a close friendship with an old couple, or a Ph.D. candidate with a blue-collar worker.

Most of these principles are obvious, but human logic and wisdom alone will fail. God never fails; therefore, prayer is the most essential step. God will help match those best suited to each other. We have experienced God's miraculous direction as we have asked him to direct and protect the pairings.

We have observed that Americans with no crosscultural background are often shy and awkward in their initial attempt to get acquainted with their newly assigned international friends. Even though they have volunteered, they may never make that first contact without encouragement or the help of a more experienced American to introduce them to each other.

Having a get-together of many newly formed pairs early in their relationship is useful. It provides them with a place to go together, the students like to meet other Americans, everyone relaxes more in a group situation, and the atmosphere from the Christians in the group is a powerful witness. It is a good time for the Americans to identify that they are Christians, if they have not already done so. The non-Christians see a sameness in each of the Americans. They see a quality they have not

observed in their other American contacts. This spirit can be
identified to them as the Spirit of Jesus Christ (if this seems
appropriate by their response or interest).

Fanning the Flame
The flame of friendship ignited during the early stages of contact could be kept burning through some of these activities:

1. Contact your friends regularly and frequently by phone,
note or personal visit. Keep in close touch.

2. Try to discover their birthdays and send a greeting or plan
a special get-together on that date.

3. Go to sports events, concerts or plays together. Explain
what is going on in unfamiliar games.

4. Do things with, not for, international students.

5. Ask if they would like to prepare a typical meal from their
country in your kitchen. They'll need your utensils and help in
buying the necessary items. This can be a wonderful experience for the whole family and a good opportunity for international students to do something with you.

6. Go for a drive to sightsee or orient them to the community.

7. Take them with you on family weekends or holidays.

8. Include them in community or family activities.

9. Ask your friends if you can bring your international friend
to their special event: shower, wedding, graduation, funeral,
birthday, picnic and so on.

10. Participate in events on campus designed for international students.

11. Introduce international students to your friends and
meet their friends. Always speak well of the international
students. Pronounce their names with proper respect, carefully
and accurately in introductions to others.

12. Your friends may enjoy a tour of your home or of a
friend's house. They may have many questions about items
unfamiliar to their culture. They may be interested in your
central heating system. Be sensitive to the fact that often
Americans are viewed as materialistic.

13. Ask friends to contact your international student friends when you are away and invite them to join some activity.

14. Your presence at your friends' graduation will be most meaningful to them. Also, any photographs will be valuable to them and their families, especially if the families are unable to attend.

15. Play family games. Look at picture albums and slides.

Guidelines on Hospitality

Personal friendships between American families or individuals and international students could be fostered through the practice of hospitality. Emphasis on hospitality is a feature of the training provided by the Taussigs. They stress that the first invitation extended to international guests is the most strategic. Reactions arising from this first meeting may well influence the entire future relationship between Americans and their overseas guests.

The Taussigs provide these guidelines on how to practice hospitality:

1. Pray. Prayer is essential. "Pray at all times in the Spirit, with all prayer and supplication" (Eph 6:18). Begin by praying that you will know how to be their friend—and that they will know how to respond to your friendship and be your friend.

2. For the first contact, an informal visit or meal together is better than an elaborate dinner or a situation with unfamiliar customs. If possible, find out if your friends have any dietary restrictions. For example, Muslims do not eat pork. Chicken and vegetables are usually acceptable to all.

Refreshments, tea or a cold drink, offered when students arrive will make them feel more at home. This is a custom in many countries. Sometimes offers must be made several times. In their country it may be considered impolite to accept the first or second time the offer is made.

3. Following up any verbal invitation with a written note is greatly appreciated by your guests. In the note clarify the exact date, time, place and how they will get there. Any of this may

have been misunderstood. The note will also serve as a reminder.

4. Always let students know in advance about how long the visit or activity will last.

5. Write down your name, address and phone number as well as the names of your family members. This will help tremendously. If you have a pet, include its name too.

6. International students' names may seem impossible to pronounce, but if you will practice their full names until you can say them correctly, they will be pleased. In many countries it is a matter of courtesy and respect to address persons by their surnames. Ask your friends what name they would like to be called. After you have had an opportunity to get to know one another better, you might want to ask permission to call them by their first name.

7. During your first visit, make arrangements for when you will see them again. This is important in many cultures and will assure the students of your acceptance of them. Tell them you enjoyed their visit.

8. In making arrangements for the next visit, be specific on date and time. Avoid the vague invitation, "Come over anytime." Most foreign visitors do not know how to interpret this. If you cannot be specific, then indicate that you will call them within a given time to make plans.

9. Find out what hours they are available for phone calls. Tell them what hours you are available to be called.

10. Try to be aware of their "free" time and avoid visits when they are busy.

11. When students are in your home for a meal, say it is your custom to give thanks for food and then say grace. After dinner, if it is your custom, read a passage of Scripture (in a modern version, if possible) and perhaps make one or two comments about it, and discuss any questions that may arise. This is not the time to preach a sermon. Then you may follow this with prayer, without singling out your friends and praying for their conversion. However, it would be well to pray for them, that

their work may be successful and that their families may be preserved and blessed of God in every way.

12. Host more than one international student at a time—it takes the pressure off any one student, and it makes him or her feel less alone.

13. Children and grandchildren prove a great asset in making friends comfortable and relaxed.

Both you and your international student friends need to be aware of each other's time limitations. "There is a time for everything, and a season for every activity under heaven" (Eccles 3:1 NIV).

International students appreciate knowing when and how to say good-by. Studies often take precedence over social events unless they can depend on being able to leave after only a short time together.

When time conflicts prevent your getting together, make a phone call, send a card or a letter. Some students rarely get a phone call or a letter in their mailbox. A letter is tangible evidence of your friendship.

Communicating Crossculturally

Part of the Taussigs' nine-hour training seminar for Americans concerns the dos and don'ts of crosscultural communication. These are their suggestions:

1. A smile is the same in any language. Warmth and sincerity bridge cultural gaps.

2. Friendship can best be developed through conversing.

3. Avoid idioms and colloquialisms. American jokes and humor are often misunderstood. Explain anything you feel might have been misinterpreted. Let your remarks be governed by sensitivity and good judgment.

4. Do not be afraid of difficulty in communication, either over the phone or in person. Friendliness and patience, combined with genuine interest and understanding, will transcend language and other cultural barriers.

5. Asking "Do you understand?" or "What did you say?" too

often may begin to undermine your friends' self-confidence. Speaking slowly and distinctly will aid them in understanding. They may hesitate to admit that they do not understand what is said. Learn to watch for signs of lack of comprehension. If you feel they did not understand, repeat the sentence using other words.

6. Locate your friends' countries on the map and read about the educational and political systems, the people and the current situation in their countries to help you feel more at ease in conversation. It takes time, concentration and unselfishness to build friendships. Communicate a sincere respect for the customs and cultures of your friends.

7. Although you may disagree with the politics of their countries, be very slow to criticize. You may not fully understand, but you can accept each other as individuals. Be proud of your country, but do not consider your way superior. Do not endeavor to speak for all Americans. While it is not always possible to understand another person, particularly one whose culture is different, acceptance of that person is possible.

8. Don't pry into finances or politics. Getting financially involved is usually unwise. Refer financial, legal or governmental matters to others.

9. Your friends will be pleased to teach you greetings in their language. Learn how to say *hello, good-by, welcome* and special greetings for significant days of celebration in their countries. In turn, tell them about *Merry Christmas, Happy New Year* and other greetings.

10. Point out that Americans often ignore each other. They are usually not discriminating against the students when they give no greeting.

11. Be patient if time does not mean the same to your friends as it does to Americans. Theirs may not be a time-controlled culture. Discuss time differences and expectations.

12. Use the phone and mail to relay bits of news, future invitations or just to chat. This solidifies relationships. The students will know they have not been forgotten and will not

be isolated in their loneliness when you are unable to be together. If you go out of town, let them know. They will understand the reason for your absence better than they would understand not hearing from you. If you move, leave your number and address with them. Send them notes from out of town so they know they are not forgotten.

Listening and Learning

Part of the art of communicating crossculturally has to do with listening and learning. Here are some pointers from the Taussigs:

1. Be a good listener, as it opens the way for a deeper friendship. Intent listening helps overcome any inability to understand a heavy accent.

2. Encourage your friends to talk about themselves, their families, their countries. This is therapy for their loneliness, and also teaches you about foreign cultures. Suggestions: "Tell me about your family. How many sisters and brothers do you have?" "How do people greet one another in your country?" "What are your mealtime customs?" "We've heard so much about [a person in the news or current events from that country]. Can you tell us more?"

Keep the conversation positive: "What do you like . . . ?" rather than "What don't you like . . . ?" "What do you know about Christianity?" "Have you ever read the Bible?" "Have you known any Christians before?"

3. Don't always ask questions. Share a little about yourself, your family and your work.

4. Ask what family games their people play, what holidays they observe and how they are observed. If possible, participate in these holidays with your friends.

5. Learn from them about their professions and goals.

6. Participate in activities with their friends and their national group.

7. Listen to tapes of music they like. They may be able to teach you a dance.

8. Ask to see their photo albums of their families. Learn the names of members of their families.

9. Go to slide shows on their countries. They may have slides they can show you.

The Circle of Impact Widens

The Taussigs began in a small, hesitant way. There was no grandiose plan, no master strategy, no knowledge of other international student ministries, no training program for American volunteers. There was only a couple who wanted to do something for international students, especially Nigerians, at Kansas State University. They have certainly made an impact.

James Hassan, who was one of a hundred and twenty Nigerian students at Kansas State, said, "Nigerian culture is very different from American culture. Back home I'm used to talking to anybody. But nobody cares about me here. I show a friendly face, but I get the impression that I'm not wanted. Some seem to say, 'What business have you got with me?' " He added, "I'm referring to American students and adults alike. But I see a spirit of brotherhood in Dr. Taussig. They [the Taussigs] are among the people who care."

Hassan was majoring in agriculture journalism. He had joined government service in 1960 and was a senior officer in the Nigerian Ministry of Agriculture, then on study leave. His wife, Rifkatu, was also an Agriculture Ministry officer. She was a senior in Kansas State majoring in home economics. Both were Christians before coming to the United States.

Korean Nam-In Kim taught crop physiology at Gang Weon National University, South Korea. When he arrived on campus, he was single and a non-Christian. He now has a Korean wife he met in the United States and a baby boy. Baptized at Grace Baptist Church in September 1980, Kim was then the only Christian in a family of seven. Kim said, "He [Dr. Taussig] is the symbol of Christianity. When new students come to KSU and they need transportation, he has someone to pick them up. He helped me spiritually. When I stayed in the dorm, he visited me one night and gave me a book on Christian living."

Donna Davis, assistant foreign student adviser of the Kansas State Foreign Student Office, said, "HIS is the only host program in Manhattan. At the beginning of each semester, HIS meets new students at the airport to welcome them to Manhattan and gets them settled. In its ongoing American friend program, the students are matched with a single student or a family. Dr. Taussig got it started and keeps it going. You may say he is a dynamic force in the program."

News of the Taussigs' ministry has gone beyond the confines of their hometown. Moody Radio interviewed them. They have established ties with other organizations involved in international student work and have visited Missouri and California on invitations to conduct their training seminars. Dr. Taussig was also elected to the Board of the National Association for Foreign Student Affairs and is a founding executive member of the Association of Christian Ministries to Internationals.

After several years of prayer for and service among international students, the Taussigs said they are grateful to God for the opportunity to go to eighty countries without having to leave Manhattan, without needing a visa and without having to learn a foreign language. At Kansas State they have the world at their doorstep.

Appendix A:
A Biblical Basis

International students are nowhere identified as such in the Bible. But they are included in two prominent ways.

First, Scripture consistently records God's love and compassion for all the nations of the world. The Lord said in his promise to Abraham: "By you all the families of the earth shall bless themselves" (Gen 12:3). This promise was reaffirmed by Christ after his resurrection. In Acts 1:8 he stated that the scope of our task to share the gospel is worldwide: "But you shall receive power when the Holy Spirit has come upon you; and you shall be my witnesses in Jerusalem and in all Judea and Samaria and to the end of the earth." This promise and instruction carry a special emphasis as they were Jesus' final words before his ascension. We are to have a global perspective in our witness.

The day of Pentecost itself was a missionary event of worldwide scope. Jews or proselytes from every nation in the Roman Empire were gathered in Jerusalem to celebrate the festival. Their presence and participation symbolized the universal nature of, and the universal need for, the gospel.

Today on the university campus we have gatherings of people from far more nations and races than on the day of Pentecost. It is figuratively possible, in a small geographical area, to obey Christ's command to be his witnesses "in Jerusalem and in all Judea and Samaria and to the end of the earth." The traditional image of the missionary as one who travels overseas is modified by this phenomenon. Crosscultural missionary work need not be left to the "professional" missionary. As Peter points out, "You are a chosen race, a royal priesthood, a holy nation, God's own people, that you may declare the wonderful deeds of him who called you out of darkness into his marvelous light" (1 Pet 2:9). All Christians are to declare God's glory to all nations.

Second, the Bible has much to say about our attitude to and treatment of aliens, sojourners, foreigners and strangers.

God's concern for the stranger is not an isolated, passing whim or fancy. He reiterates his command in Deuteronomy 10:17-19: "For the LORD your God is God of gods and LORD of lords, the great, the mighty, and the terrible God, who is not partial and takes no bribe. He executes justice for the fatherless and the widow, and loves the sojourner, giving him food and clothing. Love the sojourner therefore; for you were sojourners in the land of Egypt." God's clear message to his people is that they are to provide for sojourners.

Strangers, aliens or foreigners are not to be mistreated or oppressed. Such conduct would do violence to God's holy nature. As God's people the Israelites were to serve as examples of his holiness. The strangers' temporary presence among them did not mean that they were to be ignored or excluded from Israel's communal activities. They were to love them. Obedience to this command would inevitably mean that strangers would be impressed by their piety.

Deuteronomy 16:11 and 14 go on to instruct the Israelites to share their religious festivals with the sojourner. Moses also instructs the Israelites thus: "Assemble the people, men, women, and little ones, and the sojourner within your towns, that they may hear and learn to fear the LORD your God, and be careful to do all the words of this law" (Deut 31:12). A New Testament exhortation on our attitude to strangers states, "Do not neglect to show hospitality to strangers, for thereby some have entertained angels unawares" (Heb 13:2).

International students are strangers and sojourners in the United States. They are not tourists who are protected from the painful and alienating knocks that come with living in a land with people, customs and a language that can be frustratingly unfamiliar.

The United States is a land of immigrants. For American Christians this suggests some broad parallels with the situation the Israelites were in. The injunction is to love the sojourner in practical ways.

Distant Neighbors Living Next Door

These injunctions on strangers and sojourners are also related to the topic of neighbors. On one occasion a lawyer asks Jesus, "Teacher, which is the great commandment in the law?" Jesus replies, "You shall love the Lord your God with all your heart, and with all your soul, and with all your mind. This is the great and first commandment. And a second is like it, You shall love your neighbor as yourself. On these two commandments depend all the law and the prophets" (Mt 22:36-40).

Both commandments make love the dominant motive of God and our neighbor.

In the parable of the good Samaritan a lawyer asks Jesus, "And who is my neighbor?" (Lk 10:29). Jesus' reply establishes several facts. First, Jesus is not concerned with the traveler's nationality. He is merely described as "a man." What matters is his need of immediate help.

Second, the nature of help the wounded man requires is not spiritual. Brutally beaten, his silent cry is for physical aid.

Third, caring for another person is costly. For the Samaritan the cost is substantial, both tangible and intangible. It includes the tending of the wounds, placing the wounded man on the beast—which means that the Samaritan has to walk the rest of the journey to the inn, rendering himself more vulnerable to robbers—and paying for the man's board and lodging. Time and money are precious commodities. Their value rises sharply when spent on others, then and now.

Fourth, compassion surmounts barriers. The protagonist who ungrudgingly offers his assistance is not an Israelite but a Samaritan. This is an ironical twist to the story told to a Jewish audience. Help did not come from people traditionally expected to give aid but from someone socially unrespectable.

International students in the United States are no longer distant neighbors of American Christians. They now live next door to us. Those who have just arrived in the United States are in greatest need of help. While they are not in the same physical shape as the wounded man in the good Samaritan parable, many of them may be worse off than him. They are unable to effectively articulate their helplessness—verbally or nonverbally. They are our neighbors in need of help.

Declare His Glory among the Nations

It is doubtful that the psalmist had envisioned a college or university campus when he came up with such a flourishing line: "Declare his glory among the nations" (Ps 96:3). But he undoubtedly would have rejoiced if he were to witness a gathering of so many nations on a single campus.

Psalm 96 strikes a keynote when it begins with a call to praise the LORD. Brimming with spiritual exuberance and celebration, the psalmist is acutely aware of who God is and therefore why he deserves the praise and worship of all the nations of the earth. As apostle John avers, "We love, because he first loved us" (1 Jn 4:19). In his gospel he states, "For God so loved the world that he gave his only Son, that whoever believes in him should not perish but have eternal life. For God sent the Son into the world, not to condemn the world, but that the world might be saved through him" (Jn 3:16-17).

The desire to "sing to the LORD a new song" and to "tell of his salvation from day to day" (Ps 96:1-2) is planted in our hearts only after we know God, acknowledge our sinfulness, accept his salvation and worship him. An atmosphere of praise and worship sets the context for declaring God's glory among the nations.

Appendix B:
Organizations with International Student Ministries

An awareness of the presence of the international student community in the United States and of the need to reach out to them has increased in recent years in several ways. First, new organizations have been formed that attempt to help the international student. Second, more churches have asked for information on how to embark on a crosscultural ministry where they are. Third, more conferences on how to minister to international students have been organized by churches and parachurch organizations to encourage Christians to begin a ministry or strengthen their existing work.

Listed here are some of the organizations and churches which are members of the Association of Christian Ministries to Internationals. A brief description of their objectives is included. Most of these organizations have materials on how to minister to international students.

Al-Nour.
Jadallah Ghrayyeb, Director, P.O. Box 985, Colorado Springs, CO 80901.
Americans Meeting Internationals.
Viju Abraham/Mr. Dell McDonald, Coordinators, AMI, 2754 South Utica, Denver, CO 80236. AMI's two main objectives are to provide international students with wholesome contact and interaction with Americans, and to share Christian love through introducing international students to loving Christians.
Association of Christian Ministries to Internationals.
Art Everett, Executive Director, ACMI, P.O. Box 1775, Colorado Springs, CO 80901. ACMI is a network of Christians whose purpose is to strengthen and

encourage the development of Christian ministries to internationals temporarily residing in North America. Its objectives are fourfold. First, to provide a context for Christians to share concerns for internationals through encouraging a fellowship of prayer and to provide opportunities for interaction at local, regional and national levels. Second, to promote awareness of needs and opportunities for ministry to internationals through identifying areas of specific needs of internationals, identifying geographic locations of greatest need and informing North American Christians of present opportunities for service. Third, to plan, promote and conduct conferences for fellowship, inspiration and training of Christians ministering to internationals through sponsoring national and regional conferences, and to provide other conference organizers with resources upon request. Fourth, to develop a network for sharing materials and personnel resources through identifying all existing ministries, encouraging those concerned with placing staff in an area to communicate with existing ministries in that area, disseminating information regarding position openings and available personnel, providing information regarding existing resources, and communicating information about new resources as they emerge.

Qualifications for membership are: agreement with ACMI's statements of faith and of purpose, involvement in a Christian ministry to internationals, minimum age of eighteen, and payment of dues currently established by ACMI.

Campus Crusade for Christ.
International Ministries, CCC, Arrowhead Springs, San Bernardino, CA 92414. CCC's International Student Ministries reaches out to and disciples international students through Discovery and Action Groups. A key conference for international students is the World Opportunities Conference where the students are challenged with worldwide ministry and missions opportunities.

Christmas International House.
CIH, Coordinating Office, Room 304-A, 341 Ponce de Leon Ave., NE, Atlanta, GA 30365. CIH, run by the Presbyterians, is a two-week Christmas program (usually from December 18 to January 2) organized for international students in college or graduate school. Students may apply regardless of their race, nationality, religious background or marital status. Some programs are able to accommodate married couples with children. Application forms are usually available from the Foreign Student Advisers of the college or university.

Christmas International Houses are located in about fifty cities across the United States. Different groups or churches sponsor the program in each city. International students are guests of the local community. Room and board are free. The only cost the student has to pay is a ten-dollar application fee and the round-trip transportation to and from the CIH host community, unless extra expenses are indicated by the individual programs. Entertainment varies with each community. Programs usually include recreation, parties, movies, some television, Ping-Pong, visits in American homes, tours, time for the students to improve their English, discussions, sightseeing, relaxation and opportunities to celebrate Christmas with American families.

Among the reasons for sponsoring a CIH are a concern to provide a place for international students to go to when otherwise they would be in an empty dormitory on a deserted campus, a desire to share the Christmas holidays with people from other countries, and an interest in crosscultural experiences and international relations. Christians celebrate the birth of Jesus Christ and share with others the joy of God's love for all people during Christmas. Many churches and communities find CIH an appropriate way to enable international students to participate in the holiday season with families.

Friendship for Overseas College and University Students.
Joseph Sabounji, FOCUS Coordinator, Park Street Church, One Park St., Boston, MA 02108. FOCUS is a worldwide friendship program at Park Street Church serving international students in the Boston area. Its primary objective is to build and strengthen the church around the world by reaching and teaching internationals in the Boston area. Its goals are to establish contact with internationals, to build confident relationships, to evangelize through practical means, to train Christian internationals in discipleship and leadership, and to motivate and train American Christians to reach internationals.

Helping International Students.
Dr. & Mrs. Charles Bascom, Directors, HIS, Grace Baptist Church, 2901 Dickens Ave., Manhattan, KS 66502. HIS, sponsored by Grace Baptist Church, has five objectives. First, to help international students adjust to the American culture and develop friendships with American Christians. Second, to provide international students with the opportunity for warm Christian fellowship, for spiritual growth and maturity in their personal walk with the Lord. Third, to provide international students with an opportunity to hear a faithful, intelligent presentation of the gospel of Jesus Christ given in the power of the Holy Spirit. Fourth, to provide a valid crosscultural social vehicle where Americans can gain an understanding and appreciation of other cultures and peoples. Fifth, to have the church fellowship participate in foreign missions by sharing the love of Christ with men and women who have come to the United States from other lands.

International Friendships, Inc.
Phil Saksa, Director, IFI, 3047 Rightmire Blvd., Columbus, OH 43221. IFI seeks to reach out to international students at Ohio State University through friendship families. These families are intended to serve as a dynamic link between the international student and the American community. The

objectives of IFI members are: to share their lives and become friends with international students, to share the gospel of Jesus Christ with these students, and to ask God for students who will become committed and effective Christians in their country.

International Students, Inc.

Hal Guffey, President, ISI, P.O. Box C, Colorado Springs, CO 80901. The purposes of ISI are to assist in the planting of the church where it has never been established and to help strengthen the church where it presently exists, through internationals. ISI seeks to fulfill its vision primarily by using the following means on a worldwide scale: (1) befriending internationals while they are away from their own country; (2) evangelizing internationals using carefully planned crosscultural approaches; (3) awakening Christian internationals to their opportunities to reach other internationals for Christ, and assisting them to do so; (4) discipling Christian internationals that they, in turn, may become disciple makers; (5) teaching and training Christian internationals to prepare them for Christian service when they return to their own countries; (6) encouraging Christian internationals to return to their own countries, and assisting them through long-term follow-up services; (7) motivating local Christians to become involved with internationals in their homes and through their local churches; (8) providing training for local Christians so that they may carry on this ministry more effectively; (9) encouraging and assisting in the establishment of international student ministries in educational centers around the world; (10) assisting Christians in other countries, as fellow members of the body of Christ, to meet their physical and spiritual needs.

Inter-Varsity Christian Fellowship.

Ned Hale, Associate Director, IVCF, 233 Langdon, Madison, WI 53703. Four reasons for a special IVCF ministry to international students are given. First, they need to hear the truth of Christianity and experience the love of Christians before they can judge the claims of Christ. Second, some of these students are from countries that are closed to American Christians. The only way to get God's Word into these nations is through the citizens of the country. Third, many of these students will be going back to influential positions in government, business and education. A new relationship with Christ, or at the least, a positive attitude toward Christians, could greatly affect the course of history. Fourth, while they are here these students are lonely, as they are strangers in the American culture. They need friends and benefit much from the love of Christian friends. Such genuine friendships will influence their consideration of the gospel.

IVCF reaches these students through (1) encouraging students in I-V chapters to befriend these people who may otherwise be without American friends; (2) inviting them to activities, such as dinners, outings and other social events; (3) hosting evangelistic Bible studies tailored especially for foreigners who were not raised in Christian cultures and may have many questions; (4) inviting these students to join Thanksgiving and Christmas celebrations, which give them a chance to better understand Christianity as well as be part of a holiday where they experience the love of Jesus; (5) teaching I-V students sensitivity in relating to the international student.

Inter-Varsity Christian Fellowship—Canada.
Jim Berney, Director, 745 Mount Pleasant Road, Toronto, Ont. M4S 2N5, Canada.

Iranian Christians International, Inc.
Ebrahim Ghaffari, Director, P.O. Box 2415, Ann Arbor, MI 48106.

Mennonite Services to International Students.
Gerald Miller, Director, MSIS, 3636 16th St., NW #B1265, Washington, DC 20010. MSIS, an information and hospitality service for international students in the Washington area, is a cooperative effort among Mennonite churches to minister to the day-to-day needs of the students. MSIS's objectives are: to broaden the cultural outlook of Americans by experiencing international friendships, to strengthen the faith of Christian international students during their residence in Washington, and to love and reach out to non-Christian international students.

Navigators.
Contact Nate Mirza, 5810 Suffolk Rd., Madison, WI 53711.

Southern Baptist International Student Ministries.
Nell Magee, Consultant, National Student Ministries, 127 Ninth Avenue, North, Nashville,TN 37234. International Student Ministries is the program of Southern Baptists for ministering to the needs of international college and university students and their families through the department of National Student Ministries of the Baptist Sunday School Board. This work is done primarily on campuses by Baptist Student Unions and through local churches, with programming also at state, regional and national levels.

NSM has a full-time consultant in ISM whose responsibility is to work with state and local directors of Baptist student ministries in planning and conducting a ministry to international students. This consultant is also available to assist local church groups in ISM and to work directly with other Southern Baptist agencies for the coordination of their ministry.

ISM may vary with different groups and campuses, depending on what is done by those who are interested in internationals, who care about them and who make friends with them. The objectives are to: (1) encourage greater appreciation for and understanding of persons of different nationalities, cultures, races and religions; (2) establish sustained and meaningful relationships with international students and with any accompanying family members; (3) assist internationals in their adjustment to and in their understanding of American cultural differences; (4) provide opportunity for internationals to learn about and to experience American family life; (5) provide opportunity for exchanging religious beliefs and sharing a Christian witness with the interested non-Christian international; (6) provide opportunity for growth in commitment and discipleship of the Christian international; (7) provide a channel of contact for international students when coming to the United States and upon returning to their home countries. Friendship International House is a two-week Christmas program organized for international students.

World-Wide Students.
Cecil O'Dell II, Pastor of International Student Ministries, Grace Brethren Church, 3590 Elm Ave., Long Beach, CA 90807. World-Wide Students is a ministry of Grace Brethren Church. Its three objectives are: to evangelize and disciple international students, to provide missions training for their missions candidates, and to train internationals to be disciplers in their own countries.

Appendix C:
International Student
Statistics

Data from the United Nations Educational, Scientific and Cultural Organization show that the United States hosted almost one-third of 842,705 international students in forty-five countries in 1978.[1] Its total of 263,940 students is more than twice that of the second-largest host country, France (108,286). The Soviet Union, United Kingdom and Federal Republic of Germany each reported about 60,000 students.

Statistics from the Institute of International Education provide further perspectives into this large category of students in the United States. Rapid increases in the international student population have been reported in recent years. There were only about 34,000 students in the 1954/55 academic year. The figure rose to more than 100,000 for the first time in 1966/67. It doubled ten years later. 1980/81 saw the rapid rise to more than 300,000. There were 336,990 students in 1982/83.[2]

A majority of students in 1982/83 (119,650) came from South and East Asia.[3] This region also shows a pattern of steep increases in the number of students (see figure 1).[4] Eighteen countries had more than 5,000 students in the United States (see table 1).[5] The three leading countries with the largest percentage increase in students between 1981/82 and 1982/83 are Malaysia (9,420 to 14,070), China (4,350 to 6,230) and Republic of Korea (8,070 to 11,360).[6]

Seventy colleges and universities in the United States had more than 1,000 students out of which eighteen had more than 2,000 (see table 2).[7] The ten states with the highest international student enrollment are given in table 3.[8] And twenty universities had a hundred or more nations on their campuses. American University and Boston University led with 116 nations each.[9]

The personal characteristics of these students show that they were typically male (70.9 per cent), unmarried (80.1 per cent), primarily on personal and family funding (67.8 per cent), and holding F visas (84 per cent).[10] Approximately one in every six international students in the United States was seeking a master's degree and one in twelve was working toward a doctorate.[11]

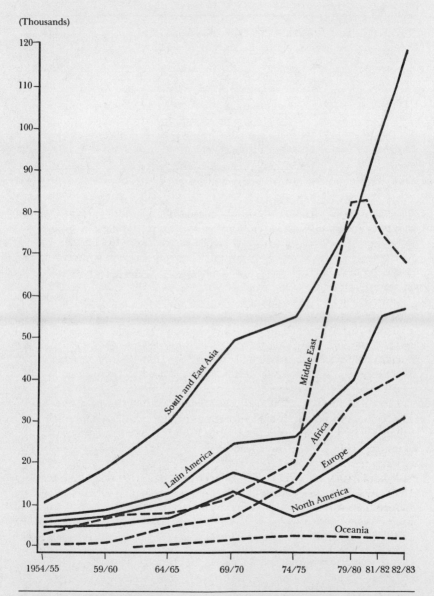

(Thousands)

Figure 1 Foreign Students in the United States by Region of Origin, Selected Years, 1954/55-1982/83. *Reprinted with permission from* Open Doors 1982/83, *an annual publication of the Institute of International Education.*

Table 1 Countries with More Than 5,000 International Students in the United States, 1982/83

Country	Students	Country	Students
Iran	26,760	Saudi Arabia	9,250
Taiwan	20,770	Hong Kong	8,610
Nigeria	20,710	Mexico	7,260
Venezuela	15,490	Lebanon	7,110
Malaysia	14,070	Jordan	6,820
Canada	14,020	Thailand	6,800
Japan	13,610	China	6,230
India	12,890	United Kingdom	5,880
Republic of Korea	11,360	Indonesia	5,030

Taken from Douglas R. Boyan, ed., Open Doors: 1982/83: Report on International Educational Exchange *(New York: Institute of International Education, 1984), p. 25.*

Table 2 Institutions with 2,000 or More International Students, 1982/83

Institution	Students	International Student Percentage of Total Enrollment
Miami-Dade Community College	4,186	11.2
University of Southern California	3,651	12.4
University of Texas, Austin	2,944	6.1
Columbia University	2,824	12.5
University of Wisconsin, Madison	2,680	6.3
George Washington University	2,568	13.4
University of Michigan, Ann Arbor	2,396	6.8
Southern Illinois University, Carbondale	2,319	9.8
Ohio State University, Main Campus	2,262	4.2
University of Minnesota, Twin Cities	2,212	3.4
Boston University	2,187	7.8
Louisiana State University, Baton Rouge	2,109	6.8
Oklahoma State University, Main Campus	2,101	9.0
Texas Southern University	2,093	25.2
University of Miami	2,063	14.1
University of California, Los Angeles	2,054	5.9
State University of New York at Buffalo, Main Campus	2,051	8.7
Northeastern University	2,050	5.3

Taken from Douglas R. Boyan, ed., Open Doors: 1982/83: Report on International Educational Exchange *(New York: Institute of International Education, 1984), p. 72.*

Table 3 States with the Highest International Student Enrollment, 1982/83

State	Students	State	Students
California	49,715	Illinois	13,781
New York	29,073	Michigan	12,771
Texas	26,577	Ohio	12,001
Florida	17,394	Pennsylvania	11,021
Massachusetts	16,075	District of Columbia	10,536

Taken from Douglas R. Boyan, ed., Open Doors: 1982/83: Report on International Educational Exchange *(New York: Institute of International Education, 1984), p. 53.*

Notes

Introduction: Opening Hearts and Doors to Internationals

[1] Mark Hanna, "The Great Blind Spot in Missions Today," World Missions Conference at Park Street Church, Boston, Massachusetts, 1975.

[2] *Statistical Yearbook 1981* (Paris: UNESCO, 1981), III, 461-91.

Chapter 1: Adjusting to a New Culture

[1] Kalervo Oberg, "Culture Shock: Adjustment to the New Cultural Environments," *Practical Anthropology* 7, no. 4 (1960):177.

[2] William A. Smalley, "Culture Shock, Language Shock, and the Shock of Self-Discovery," *Practical Anthropology* 10, no. 2 (1963):49.

[3] Personal interview with William C. Hill, assistant dean of students, Wheaton College Graduate School, 3 January 1983.

[4] Personal interview with Stephen T. Franklin, professor of theology, Wheaton College Graduate School, 6 December 1982.

[5] Smalley, "Culture Shock," p. 49.

[6] Ibid.

[7] Oberg, "Culture Shock," p. 178.

[8] Ibid., pp. 178-79.

[9] Louis J. Luzbetak, *The Church and Cultures* (Techny, Ill.: Divine Word Publications, 1963), pp. 96-100.

[10] Smalley, "Culture Shock," pp. 55-56.

[11] Personal interview with Robert Taussig, professor of veterinary medicine, Kansas State University, 20 March 1982.

[12] Eugene A. Nida, *Customs and Cultures* (New York: Harper & Brothers, 1954), pp. 8-9.

[13] Richard Ostling, "The New Missionary," *Time,* 27 December 1982.

[14]Nida, *Customs,* p. 1.

Chapter 2: Academic and Social Needs

[1]"Confucian Work Ethic," *Time,* 28 March 1983, p. 52.

[2]As editor of *Impact* magazine, a Singapore publication, I had received mail from Christian publishing houses in the United States which addressed my letters and packages to a variety of countries: "Singapore, Japan," "Singapore, China," and "Singapore, Indonesia." It should be "Singapore, Republic of Singapore."

[3]On reflection, I believe I could have misread the cultural cues when I met the registrar in his office. He is an American and his mannerisms could possibly have been interpreted by an American student as perfectly normal banter. In my early days in the United States, when I was in a disoriented state, I failed to decipher that. My account in the text is a record of how I felt as the events unfolded.

[4]Education and World Affairs Committee on Foreign Student Affairs, *The Foreign Student: Whom Shall We Welcome?* (New York: Education and World Affairs, 1964), p. 6.

[5]Personal interview with J. Julius Scott, Jr., chairman of the Theological Studies Dept., Wheaton College Graduate School, 7 December 1982.

[6]Marvin K. Mayers, *Christianity Confronts Culture* (Grand Rapids, Mich.: Zondervan Publishing House, 1964), p. 6.

[7]Edward T. Hall, *Beyond Culture* (Garden City: Anchor Press/Doubleday, 1976), p. 115.

[8]Irwin T. Sanders and Jennifer C. Ward, *Bridges to Understanding* (New York: McGraw-Hill, 1970), p. 147.

[9]Seth Spaulding and Michael J. Flack, *The World's Students in the United States: A Review and Evaluation of Research on Foreign Students* (New York: Praeger Publishers, 1976), p. 290.

[10]W. Frank Hull IV, *Foreign Students in the United States of America: Coping Behavior within the Educational Environment* (New York: Praeger Publishers, 1978), pp. 35-44.

[11]Personal interview with James E. Plueddemann, dean of Wheaton College Graduate School, 15 December 1982.

[12]Telephone interview with Yi-Qiang Xiong, 24 March 1982.

[13]Lawson Lau, "A Conference with 'Real People,' " *Leadership 100,* July-August 1983, p. 21.

Chapter 3: Overcoming Cultural Barriers

[1]B. Schrieke, *Alien Americans: A Study of Race Relations* (New York: The Viking Press, 1936), pp. 3-22.

[2]Gregory Razran, "Ethnic Dislikes and Stereotypes: A Laboratory Study," *The*

Journal of Abnormal and Social Psychology, 45 (1950):7-27.
[3]Interview, Franklin.
[4]Interview, Taussig.
[5]Mayers, *Christianity Confronts Culture,* pp. 149-54.
[6]Lawson Lau, "Why Foreign Students Usually Hate the United States," *Christianity Today,* 21 May 1982, pp. 30-31.
[7]Interview, Plueddemann. Professor Plueddemann worked in Nigeria for thirteen years with the Evangelical Churches of West Africa.
[8]Mayers, *Christianity Confronts Culture,* pp. 148-49.
[9]Hall, *Beyond Culture,* pp. 91-101.
[10]Interview, Plueddemann.

Chapter 4: The Crucial Contact
[1]Thom Hopler, *A World of Difference: Following Christ Beyond Your Cultural Walls* (Downers Grove, Ill.: InterVarsity Press, 1981), pp. 105-6.
[2]Abraham H. Maslow, *Motivation and Personality,* 2nd ed. (New York: Harper & Row, 1970), pp. 35-47.
[3]Interview, Taussig.
[4]Ellie McGrath, "Confucian Work Ethic," *Time,* 28 March 1983, p. 52.
[5]Paul Tournier, *The Meaning of Persons* (New York: Harper & Brothers, 1957), p. 143.
[6]Ibid.
[7]Paul F. Barkman, Edward R. Dayton, and Edward L. Gruman, *Christian Collegians and Foreign Missions* (Monrovia: Missions Advanced Research & Communications Center, 1969), p. 50.
[8]Mayers, *Christianity Confronts Culture,* pp. 68-76.
[9]Joseph Fletcher, *Situation Ethics* (Philadelphia: The Westminster Press, 1966), p. 26.
[10]Mayers, *Christianity Confronts Culture,* pp. 71-72.
[11]Harvie M. Conn, *Evangelism: Doing Justice and Preaching Grace* (Grand Rapids, Mich.: Zondervan Publishing House, 1982), p. 44.
[12]Ibid.
[13]Ibid., p. 45.
[14]Ibid.
[15]Paul E. Little, *A Guide to International Friendship* (Madison, Wis.: Inter-Varsity Christian Fellowship, 1959), p. 7.
[16]Ibid.

Chapter 5: Proclaiming the Gospel
[1]Geoffrey E. W. Scobie, *Psychology of Religion* (New York: John Wiley & Sons, 1975), p. 51.
[2]C. S. Lewis, ed. *George MacDonald: An Anthology* (New York: Macmillan

Publishing Co., Inc., 1947), p. xxxiii.

[3]Ibid.

[4]Ibid.

[5]Ibid.

[6]Ibid.

[7]Ibid.

[8]Interview, Xiong.

[9]Telephone interview with Nell Magee, 26 March 1982.

[10]Charin Arayawunnikui, letter to Nell Magee, n.d.

[11]Personal interview with Joseph Bayly, 9 December 1982.

[12]Betsy R. Guffey, "Bring the World to Your Home" (Colorado Springs: International Students, Inc., n.d.), p. 1.

[13]Ibid., p. 2.

[14]John R. W. Stott, *Christian Mission in the Modern World* (Downers Grove, Ill.: InterVarsity Press, 1975), pp. 71-74.

[15]Peter Wilkes, ed., *Christianity Challenges the University* (Downers Grove, Ill.: InterVarsity Press, 1981).

[16]Ibid., p. 13.

[17]Ibid.

[18]See *Eerdmans' Handbook to Christian Belief* (Grand Rapids, Mich.: Wm. B. Eerdmans Publishing Company, 1982) for a concise introduction to basic Christian belief.

Chapter 6: *Proselytize* Is a Dirty Word

[1]*Standards and Responsibilities in International Educational Interchange* (Washington, D.C.: National Association for Foreign Student Affairs, 1979).

[2]*Guidelines for Members* (Colorado Springs: Association of Christian Ministries to Internationals).

[3]Brent Waters and Dennis Peterson, "Religious Groups and International Students," *NAFSA Newsletter* 34, no. 4 (4 February 1983): 77, 92-93.

[4]Interview, Bayly.

[5]Stott, *Christian Mission*, p. 126.

[6]Personal interview with Ned Hale, 16 December 1982.

Chapter 7: Preparing for Re-entry

[1]For a good discussion of this subject see R. Theoret, N. Adler, D. Kealy, F. Hawes, *Re-entry: A Guide for Returning Home* (Ottawa: Canadian International Development Agency, 1979).

[2]Letter received from Marvin Mardock, 9 August 1983.

[3]*Malaysian Christian Handbook,* rev. ed. (Toronto: Singaporean Malaysian Awareness Group, 1982).

[4]Ibid.

Chapter 8: The Taussigs: A Model Couple

[1]This material and substantial portions of that found on pp. 116-24 are adapted from Dr. Bob and Mary Taussig, *Helping International Students Orientation Handbook* (Manhattan, Kansas: Helping International Students, 1982), pp. 4-9, 16.

Appendix C: International Student Statistics

[1]*Statistical Yearbook 1981* (Paris: UNESCO, 1981), III, 461-91.

[2]Douglas R. Boyan, ed., *Open Doors: 1982/83* (New York: Institute of International Education, 1984), pp. 12-13.

[3]Ibid., p. 16.

[4]Ibid., p. 14.

[5]Ibid., p. 25.

[6]Ibid., p. 24.

[7]Ibid., pp. 72-73.

[8]Ibid., p. 53.

[9]Ibid., p. 75.

[10]Ibid., pp. 41-45.

[11]Ibid., p. 39.